CAMPAIGN 333

THE ALEUTIANS 1942–43

Struggle for the North Pacific

BRIAN LANE HERDER

ILLUSTRATED BY DOROTHY J. HWEE

Series editor Marcus Cowper

OSPREY PUBLISHING
Bloomsbury Publishing Plc

Kemp House, Chawley Park, Cumnor Hill, Oxford OX2 9PH, UK
29 Earlsfort Terrace, Dublin 2, Ireland
1385 Broadway, 5th Floor, New York, NY 10018, USA
Email: info@ospreypublishing.com

www.ospreypublishing.com

OSPREY is a trademark of Osprey Publishing, a division of Bloomsbury Publishing Plc.

First published in Great Britain in 2019

A CIP catalog record for this book is available from the British Library.

ISBN: PB: 978 1 4728 3254 2
ePub: 978 1 4728 3253 5
ePDF: 978 1 4728 3255 9
XML: 978 1 4728 3256 6

21 22 23 24 25 10 9 8 7 6 5 4 3

Index by Sharon Redmayne
Typeset in Myriad Pro and Sabon
Maps by www.bounford.com
3D BEVs by The Black Spot
Page layouts by PDQ Digital Media Solutions, Bungay, UK
Printed and bound in India by Replika Press Private Ltd.

Key to military symbols

XXXXX Army Group, XXXX Army, XXX Corps, XX Division, X Brigade, III Regiment, II Battalion

I Company/Battery, ••• Platoon, •• Section, • Squad, Infantry, Artillery, Cavalry

Airborne, Unit HQ, Air defense, Air Force, Air mobile, Air transportable, Amphibious

Antitank, Armor, Air aviation, Bridging, Engineer, Headquarters, Maintenance

Medical, Missile, Mountain, Navy, Nuclear, biological, chemical, Ordnance, Parachute

Reconnaissance, Signal, Supply, Transport movement, Rocket artillery, Air defense artillery

Key to unit identification

Unit identifier, Parent unit, Commander
(+) with added elements
(–) less elements

Artist's note

For further information about Dorothy J. Hwee's work, please visit:

http://www.artofdjh.blogspot.com

Author's acknowledgements

I would like to thank Tracy White at www.researcheratlarge.com for several NARA photographs, which have been most helpful.

Dedication

This book is dedicated to my maternal grandfather, Chief Boatswain's Mate Vincent S. Muscari (November 5, 1913–February 15, 1967) of Dog Company, 38th US Naval Construction Battalion (Special). A US Navy Seabee, Muscari served in the Aleutian theater as part of the 38th NCB's deployment to Kodiak, Adak, and Kiska between April 1943 and May 1944.

Author's notes

The Aleutian campaign straddled the international dateline. Events occurring in the Home Islands are given local Japanese time (East longitude date, Zone – 9). All remaining dates/times are Aleutian (Zone + 10).

Attu's most prominent coastal features had long been named (Massacre Bay refers to the 1745 cliffside slaughter of 15 native Aleuts by Russian fur traders). However, the island's interior features only received their American names after the May 1943 battle. To insure clarity, the Attu topography's post-battle American names are used throughout the narrative.

CONTENTS

Western North America commands, 1940–44

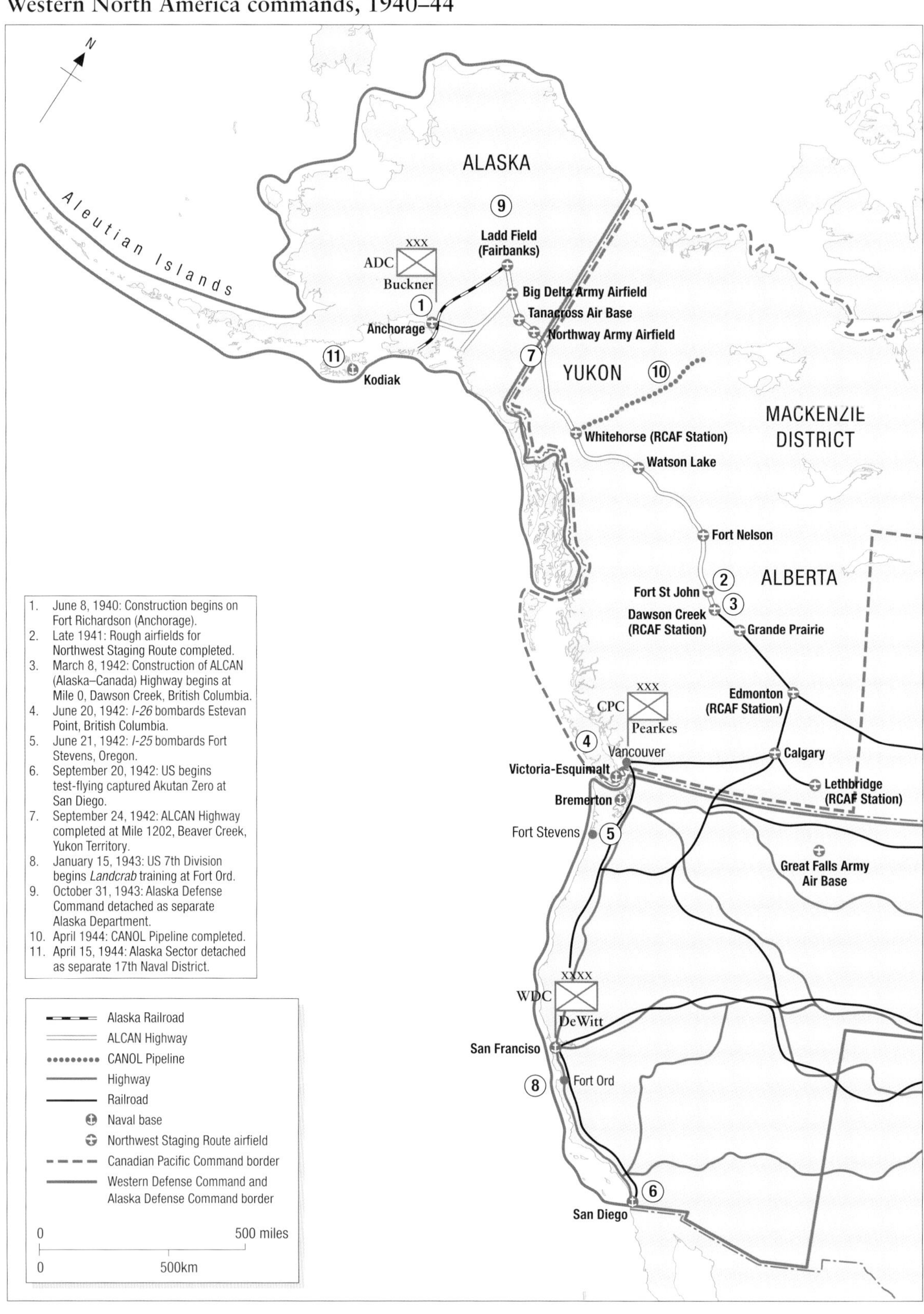

ORIGINS OF THE CAMPAIGN

ALASKA: THE STRATEGIC FRONTIER

Derided as "Seward's Folly," the United States government had purchased Alyeska from Czar Alexander II's Russian Empire on March 30, 1867 for $7.2 million. Alaskan development was sparked by the 1897 Klondike Gold Rush and sustained by subsequent gold rushes at Nome (1899–1909) and Fairbanks (1903–11). By 1912, the US federal government officially upgraded the District of Alaska to an incorporated US Territory, legally establishing Alaska and its outlying islands as an inseparable part of the United States homeland. The Snyder Act of 1924 confirmed US citizenship to all American Indians, including Alaska's indigenous Aleuts.

Alaska looms as America's vast northern wilderness of glacial fjords, alpine lakes, boreal forest, arctic tundra, active volcanoes, immense icefields, and towering mountain ranges soaring 20,310ft – North America's highest. Discovered in 1741 by Vitus Bering, Alaska's Aleutian Islands – a long, rugged, volcanic archipelago – sweep 1,200 miles west from the Alaska Peninsula toward Siberia. The bleak Aleutians are unhappily located where the warm, wet Japan Current collides with Arctic cold fronts, interminably shrouding the islands in a chill, misty gloom. The wretched climate brandishes incessant fog, freezing rains, blizzards, and violent williwaws, a unique regional windstorm reaching 140mph. The islands' barren, windswept surface is covered by tundra-crusted muskeg, a sodden, glutinous, 3ft-deep volcanic ash quagmire, rendering transportation, construction, and logistics nightmarishly difficult. The oppressive Aleutian conditions easily smother combat, movement, and human life in general.

Alaska's 1940 civilian population of 72,524 (39,740 indigenous natives) imported 90 percent of its food. Electricity was rare. Alaska possessed no overland connections, requiring freighters to navigate the 30ft tides at Anchorage, the Territory's main port. Alaska's civil air network was well established by skilled bush pilots. Surface infrastructure totaled 625 miles of railroads and 11,000 miles of primitive roads and trails, servicing a region larger than modern France, Spain, Germany, and Great Britain combined. Alaska's only all-weather route inland was the US Department of the Interior's Alaska Railroad, extending 470 miles from Seward to Fairbanks via Anchorage. Running from Valdez to Fairbanks was the Richardson Highway. The Yukon and Kuskokwim rivers were navigable for four to five months annually.

A White Pass & Yukon train headed north from Skagway, Alaska in 1899. Intended to carry traffic to the Yukon goldfields, the 3ft narrow gauge line was one of Alaska's first major infrastructure projects and today operates as a heritage railway. Modern Alaskan history arguably begins with the 1897 Klondike Gold Rush. (Eric A. Hegg/Wikimedia Commons/Public Domain)

A globe reveals Alaska lay close to all major 1941 belligerents. London, Berlin, Moscow, and "almost every other strategic northern capital" all lay within 4,000 miles of Alaska's Fairbanks, itself situated halfway between New York and Tokyo. The shortest possible flight between the United States and Japan, the great circle route, runs through Alaska.

In 1907, US Navy officer James H. Oliver imagined the Aleutians as War Plan Orange's northern flank in a Pacific-wide counter-offensive against Japan, while in 1911 and 1914 famed strategist Alfred Mahan advocated the Aleutians as the US Pacific Fleet's offensive axis. The 1922 Washington Naval Treaty banned military bases in the western Aleutians and Japan's Kurile Islands. In November 1926, the US Army–Navy Joint Planning Committee designated Alaska as Class E coastline – American territory potentially open to invasion. By 1928, flamboyant and controversial US Army pilot Brigadier-General Billy Mitchell envisioned hundreds of incendiary and poison gas-laden strategic bombers staging from Alaska through Siberia to level "the greatest aerial targets the world has ever seen" – Japan's densely populated, highly combustible wood and paper cities. Testifying in 1935, Mitchell proclaimed Alaska "the key point of the whole Pacific," telling Congress, "He who holds Alaska holds the world. It is the most strategic place in the world. It is the jumping-off place to smash Japan."

Japan withdrew from the treaty system in 1936, nullifying the Western Pacific fortification ban. Anthony Dimond, Alaska's powerless delegate to Congress, reported in 1937, "Alaska today could be taken almost overnight by a hostile force. It is today without any form of defense. At least $450 million have been spent [in Hawaii] and yet ... so far as the main body of the United States is concerned, the defense of Alaska is of much greater consequence ... What's the use of locking one door and leaving another wide open?"

By 1939, perceptive US Navy officers imagined Japan regarded Alaska as "the most dangerous of all possible directions" an American attack could come from, predicting Japan would occupy the Aleutians "at the first opportunity," creating "serious political, economic, and psychological repercussions."

FORTIFYING ALASKA, 1939–41

Increasing German and Japanese aggression shortly galvanized American interest in defending the Territory. In 1939, Congress allocated the Army Air Corps $4 million to establish the Cold Weather Test Station at Fairbanks' Ladd Field, and in September $19 million of construction began on three US Navy bases recommended by the 1938 Hepburn Board.

On April 22, 1940, American newspapers reported that US Coast Guard cutter *Perseus* had observed Nazi–Soviet forces constructing a major naval base on the Russian island of Big Diomede, just off the Alaskan coast (in fact

Alaska Defense Command, June 1942

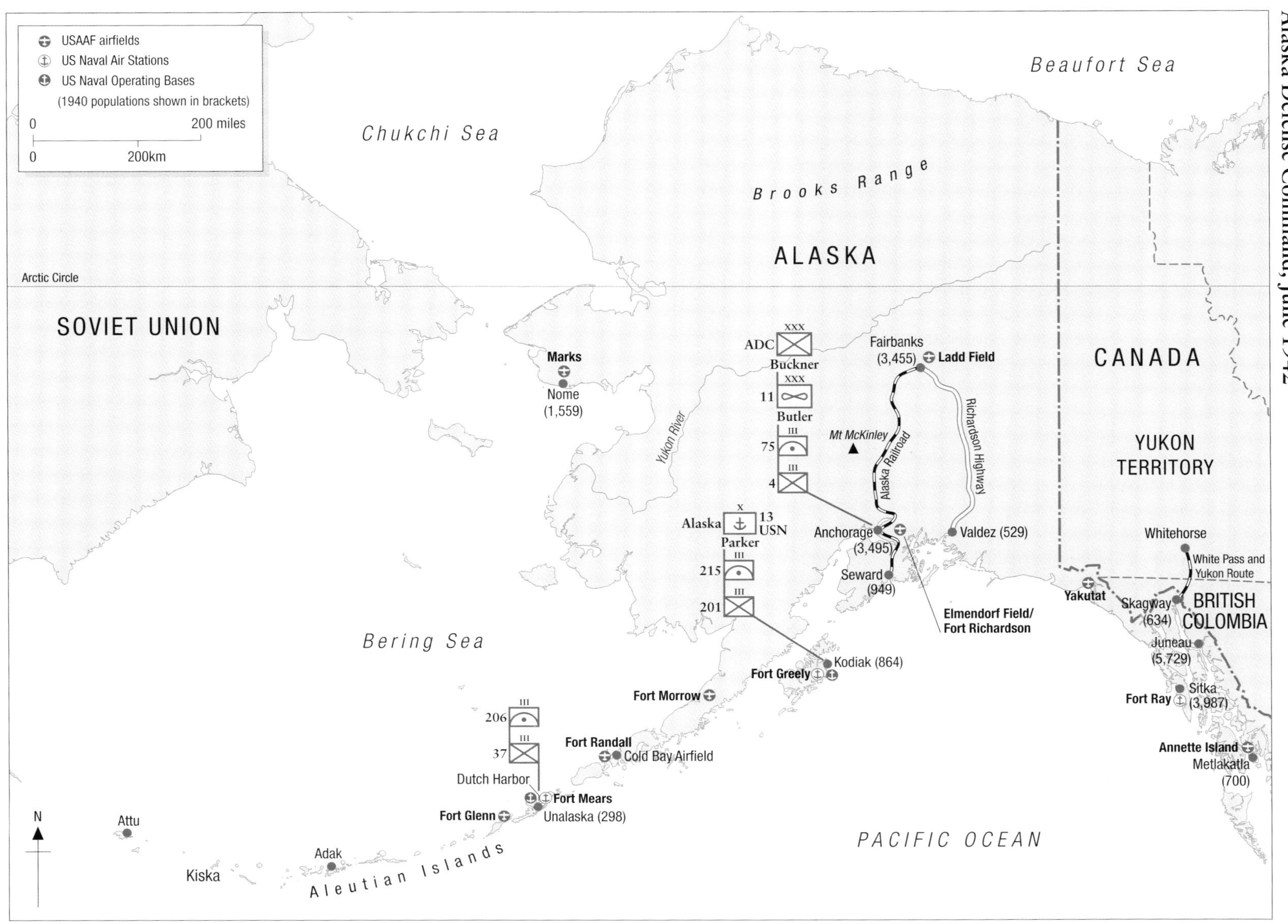

In the foreground of this 1942 Dutch Harbor painting by William F. Draper is a YP (Yard Patrol) boat – a fishing boat commandeered by the USN, painted gray, and sometimes armed with a machine gun. Moored behind it is a US submarine. Commander "Squeaky" Anderson scoffed that the YP boats "would sink if rammed by a barnacle." (Courtesy of Navy Art Collection, Naval History and Heritage Command)

it was merely a harmless science outpost). By June, the press declared a Nazi–Soviet invasion of Alaska imminent; Territorial Governor Ernest Gruening asserted, "A handful of enemy parachutists could capture Alaska overnight." Congress promptly appropriated the first of $350 million toward Alaskan defense. With world war looming, the United States ultimately adopted "Rainbow 5," the 1939 war plan concentrating maximum national power against Germany first and relegating the Pacific to an initial holding action. Rainbow 5 therefore tacitly endorsed Major-General Stanley Embick's concept of an Alaska–Hawaii–Panama "strategic triangle" as the United States' absolute Pacific defense zone.

Alaska's first combat unit, the 4th Infantry Regiment, began arriving in June 1940. Lieutenant-General John DeWitt, commander IX Corps Area (soon US Fourth Army), established the subsidiary Alaska Defense Command on June 26. Colonel Simon Bolivar Buckner, Jr was named commander. Endowed with tremendous humor, fortitude, and intellect, the indomitable 54-year-old Kentuckian arrived in Anchorage on July 22, 1940. Buckner beheld a colossal task ahead, yet enjoyed the unflagging devotion of DeWitt, who promised to support the outspoken, unorthodox Buckner "right up to the lynching."

Until 1939, the US Navy had largely ignored Alaska. Buckner opined naval officers possessed "an instinctive dread of Aleutian waters, feeling that they were inhabited by a ferocious monster that was always breathing fogs and coughing up williwaws that would blow the unfortunate mariner onto uncharted rocks and forever destroy his chances of becoming an admiral." Yet Buckner worked well with the agreeable, competent Captain Ralph C. Parker (USN), appointed October 1940 as Alaska sector commander of Seattle's Northern Coastal Frontier (13th Naval District).

Buckner was an accomplished pilot, having trained Army aviators in World War I. Recognizing Alaska's vast wilderness made airpower supreme,

Buckner's top priority was constructing an Alaskan air force and requisite infrastructure. Alaska's first combat aircraft arrived in February 1941 – 20 crated P-36 Hawk fighters of the 18th Pursuit Squadron. By July, 38 P-36s and B-18 Bolo bombers had arrived. The Alaska Defense Command Air Force was activated on October 17, 1941, briefly titled the Alaskan Air Force, and eventually redesignated the US Eleventh Air Force on February 5, 1942.

After a July 3, 1941 alert, Buckner initiated offshore USAAF patrols, outraging Washington-bound US Navy officials who deemed maritime patrol a USN mission and who additionally blocked construction of USAAF airfields in the Aleutians. On November 28, 1941, Buckner wrote US Army chief George C. Marshall, "Quick-drying cement does us very little good in speeding up construction unless quick-drying ink is used on the approval of our plans." Marshall quietly negotiated to phase USAAF patrols over to the Navy once Navy strength allowed.

Yet months earlier Buckner had personally scouted the Aleutians for islands suitable for airfields, including Umnak, Adak, Amchitka, Kiska, Shemya, and Attu. By August 1941, the fictional "Blair Fish Packing Company" had landed at Alaska Peninsula's Cold Bay and begun construction of a "cannery." Inside crates labeled Saxton & Co., Consolidated Packing Company, and Cannery Equipment lurked heavy machinery to illegally build Buckner's Aleutian airfields via funds Buckner had embezzled. On November 26, the War Department officially authorized construction of Fort Glenn airfield at Umnak's Otter Point, never discovering Buckner's illicit claim-jumping scheme.

Between June 30 and September 30, 1941, Alaska Defense Command strength had grown from 7,263 to 21,565, including four infantry regiments, three and one-half anti-aircraft regiments, a 155mm gun mobile coast artillery regiment, and a tank company. The October 16, 1941 "Joint Pacific Coastal Frontier Defense Plan, Rainbow No. 5" codified the comprehensive

A PBY Catalina overflying a wintry Aleutian island in unusually clear conditions. The notorious "Made in Japan" Aleutian weather lent itself easily to American gallows humor. When a forward-deployed PBY squadron commander received a call from his irate superior demanding to know why his planes weren't flying, the officer allegedly glanced outside at the 100mph blizzard and deadpanned, "The only thing flying out here is Quonset huts." (Naval History and Heritage Command)

US plan for Alaskan defense. Additionally, the Canadian government collaborated to help construct the Northwest Staging Route to Alaska through Alberta, British Columbia, and Yukon Territory. Five airfields were partially operational by December 1941. Prime Minister Mackenzie King's government also acquiesced to American construction of the Alcan (Alaska-Canadian) highway and Canol petroleum pipeline, which President Roosevelt would authorize on February 11 and April 29, 1942.

THE NORTH PACIFIC SITUATION, 1941–42

In May 1939, Japanese–Soviet skirmishes on the Manchuria–Mongolia border had escalated into undeclared war. By August 31, the Soviet-Mongolian 1st Army Group under Komkor (Lieutenant-General) Georgy Zhukov had decisively defeated Japan's Kwantung Army, militarily and politically humiliating the Imperial Japanese Army (IJA) leadership. The Nomonhan Incident (Khalkhyn Gol) ended Japanese ambitions of invading the Soviet Union or endorsing the IJA's northern strategy, precipitating monumental consequences.

On September 27, 1940, Japan signed the Tripartite Pact with Germany and Italy. The following year, on June 22, 1941, Japan's nominal new allies invaded the Soviet Union. Yet two days later, Imperial General Headquarters (IGHQ) issued a resolution "not intervening in the German–Soviet war for the time being" and in August 1941, Japan and the Soviet Union reaffirmed their mutual neutrality.

Though ostensibly allied with each other's mortal enemies, Japan and the Soviet Union desperately wished to avoid two-front wars. From 1941, both stiffly maintained their awkward military non-interference. However, between 1941 and 1945 the United States' Lend-Lease program would funnel 7,926 aircraft and 8.2 million tons of war materiel to the Soviet Union through Alaskan and North Pacific routes. The US government naively imagined Stalin would return American generosity by allowing US forces to stage against Japan from nearby Siberia. This inexplicable delusion assumed the Soviet Union – existentially imperiled by Nazi Germany – would indulge American convenience by risking unnecessary war with Japan 3,000 miles from the Eastern Front. The chimera of Siberian bases explains why the United States would pour disproportionately lavish wartime resources (if not combat forces) into Alaska by 1944.

In July 1940, the US government's ill-conceived Export Control Act had begun leveraging crushing American

Mongolian People's Army infantry seen advancing against the Japanese at the Battle of Khalkhyn Gol, summer 1939. Khalkhyn Gol produced a disproportionate impact on World War II by inspiring Japan to abandon its long-standing ambitions against the Soviet Union and attack the Western powers instead. Additionally, it was Khalkhyn Gol that brought Zhukov's martial talents to Stalin's attention. (Wikimedia Commons/Public Domain)

trade advantages to coerce Japan into complete withdrawal from Asia. By mid-1941, the ham-fisted American diplomacy had instead inspired Japan's ruling junta to replace vital American imports by conquering resource-rich Southeast Asia. Japan's "Southern Strategy" explicitly accepted war against Britain, the Netherlands, and the United States. Months later, the Imperial Japanese Navy's Kido Butai (carrier battle group) negotiated the gloomy, empty North Pacific well south of Buckner's sparse patrols. On December 7, 1941, the six Japanese carriers effortlessly mauled Pearl Harbor and retired undamaged.

A painting by William F. Draper of the 11th Fighter Squadron's "Aleutian Tiger" P-40s at Umnak. The 11th Fighter Squadron was commanded by Major Jack Chennault, son of Claire Chennault of Chinese "Flying Tigers" fame. The younger Chennault would eventually command the Eleventh Air Force's 343rd Fighter Group. (Courtesy of Navy Art Collection, Naval History and Heritage Command)

Hours earlier, Alaskan Air Force commander Colonel Everett Davis had observed, "By no stretch of the imagination can we ... defend the Territory against any attack in force." Contemplating Pearl Harbor, Buckner mused, "There but for the fog go I." Buckner and Gruening immediately transformed Alaska into a war zone. Alaska then hosted 22,000 US Army personnel – mostly service troops but including 2,200 USAAF personnel. The US Navy posted 180 personnel at Sitka, 300 at Kodiak, 64 at Dutch Harbor, and six PBY Catalina patrol bombers throughout Alaska. On December 11, 1941, the War Department established DeWitt's US Fourth Army area as the Western Defense Command. Within weeks, Buckner and the USAAF each requested total command of both Alaska's air and ground forces, to no avail.

Captain Parker's so-called Alaskan Navy was reinforced with World War I-era destroyers and requisitioned US Coast Guard cutters. By January 1942, six ancient S-boat submarines and ten PBY Catalinas had begun patrols from Dutch Harbor. On January 1, the USAAF dispatched 25 P-40 Warhawks and 13 B-26 Marauders to Alaska from Sacramento, California. Eleven crashed en route; only eight had arrived by January 25, confirming Buckner's assertion, "Planes cannot be rushed to Alaska."

Yet within months of Pearl Harbor, Alaska Defense Command boasted a constellation of 14 operational military bases and 30 operable USAAF and civilian airfields supporting 25,000 troops and five USAAF squadrons. Buckner wrote DeWitt, "My greatest concern now is to get a squadron of P-40s on the field at Umnak. The field is there for use by ourselves or by the enemy, whichever gets their first."

Across the Pacific, Japan's highly choreographed, brilliantly executed "First Operational Phase" had opened December 7, 1941 and triumphantly concluded March 1942, having devastated Allied Pacific power and accomplishing all pre-war aims of establishing Japanese economic self-sufficiency. On March 7, IGHQ authorized the primarily naval "Second Operational Phase," rejecting an invasion of Australia, but extending Japan's defensive perimeter deeper into the Pacific. Deriving from Combined Fleet's November 1941 Operation Order No. 1, the Second Operational Phase identified the Aleutians and Midway as "Areas [to be] occupied or destroyed as soon as the operational situations permit."

CHRONOLOGY

1942

April 20	IGHQ approves Operations *MI* and *AL*.
June 3–4	*Ryujo* and *Junyo* raid Dutch Harbor; USN destroys four Japanese carriers off Midway.
June 5	Operation *MI* canceled; Operation *AL* proceeds.
June 6/7	Japanese occupy Kiska and Attu.
June 11	First USAAF and USN air raids against Kiska ("Kiska Blitz").
August 30	US Army occupies Adak.
September 16	US Army occupies Atka.

1943

January 4	Kinkaid relieves Theobald as US North Pacific Area commander.
January 12	US Army occupies Amchitka.
March 26	US TG-16.6 repulses IJN Fifth Fleet off Komandorski Islands.
April 1	Kawase relieves Hosogaya as IJN Fifth Fleet commander.
May 11	US invades Attu in Operation *Landcrab*.
May 16	Landrum relieves Brown as US Landing Force Attu commander.
May 30	US completes liberation of Attu.
July 18	First USAAF raid against Kurile Islands.
July 28	IJN's Operation *KE* successfully evacuates Kiska garrison.
August 15–17	US–Canadian forces re-occupy empty Kiska in Operation *Cottage*.

OPPOSING COMMANDERS

JAPANESE

Twenty-eight admirals and 84 captains sortied to execute the IJN's enormous Midway–Aleutians operation, led by Combined Fleet commander **Admiral Isoroku Yamamoto**. Yamamoto had studied at Harvard and spoke fluent English; he thus held the American spirit and war-making power in much greater regard than his peers. However, Yamamoto's fatalistic personality prevented him from sufficiently protesting war with the United States. American P-38 fighters would assassinate Yamamoto over the South Pacific on April 18, 1943 as part of Operation *Vengeance*. **Admiral Mineichi Koga** would be named Combined Fleet's new commander on May 21, 1943. Koga's immediate first task was to personally lead the IJN's planned Attu relief mission, Operation *Kita*.

Admiral Isoroku Yamamoto defies easy description. Vibrant and complex, Yamamoto was most distinguished by his uniquely powerful charisma. Though a manipulative and arguably disastrous strategist, the strong-willed Yamamoto's leadership nevertheless proved impossible to replace after his April 1943 assassination. (Naval History and Heritage Command)

Vice Admiral Boshiro Hosogaya commanded the IJN's Fifth Fleet, which administered North Pacific operations – typically "the defensive patrol of the assigned area" and "anti-Soviet security." Hosogaya's assigned forces were greatly strengthened for the Aleutian campaign, where they sortied as the Northern Force. Hosogaya was eventually removed for insufficient aggressiveness. **Vice Admiral Shiro Kawase** would replace Hosogaya as Fifth Fleet commander on April 1, 1943.

Rear Admiral Kakuji Kakuta commanded Dai-ni Kido Butai (Second Mobile Force – carriers *Ryujo* and *Junyo*) during the June 1942 Dutch Harbor attack. **Commander Nifumi Mukai** led the IJN's Maizuru 3rd Special Naval Landing Force (SNLF) invasion force ashore at Kiska, which would become the IJN's primary Aleutian base under **Rear Admiral Monzo Akiyama**. Occupying Attu was the IJA 301st Independent Infantry Battalion led by **Major Matsutoshi Hozumi**.

Lieutenant-General Simon Buckner seen here in 1943 after receiving his third star. In July 1944, Buckner was promoted to US Tenth Army command. In contrast to his Alaska service, Buckner's Okinawa invasion plan proved costly and controversially unimaginative. On June 18, 1945, Buckner fell to Japanese artillery shrapnel on Okinawa, the Pacific's highest-ranking US officer killed in action. (Photo by Dmitri Kessel/The LIFE Picture Collection/Getty Images)

In August 1942, **Lieutenant-General Kiichiro Higuchi** was named commander Northern Army, which defended Hokkaido, Sakhalin, and the Kuriles. Incidentally, Higuchi had masterminded the 1938 Otpor incident, which rescued 20,000 Jewish refugees fleeing the Nazis through Manchuria. Higuchi appointed **Colonel Yasuyo Yamasaki** commander 2nd District Force, North Seas Garrison in February 1943. Yamasaki was ordered to Attu to direct its isolated defense to the bitter end, proving a brilliant defensive tactician in a hopeless situation.

US–CANADIAN

Even by US Pacific War standards, the United States' Alaskan theater command structure was appallingly byzantine and inefficient. Alaska's hostile conditions brought out the best and worst in men. Many respected American officers succumbed to the campaign's smothering adversity, but a conspicuous few, gifted with relentless psychological constitutions, shone brightly.

Alaska's internal military and civil C3 (command, communications, and control) was maintained by the Alaska Communications System (ACS). Before 1936, the ACS was known as WAMCATS, the US Army's Washington-Alaska Military Cable and Telegraph System, first operational in 1903. By 1942, the ACS' expensively maintained telegraph wires had been replaced by radio relays – frequently disrupted by Alaska's high-latitude atmospherics and augmented by couriers and dogsleds. Submarine cables connected Juneau, Sitka, and Valdez to the US mainland network at Seattle.

The Alaskan theater was unofficially a joint US–Canadian effort. On August 18, 1940, Roosevelt and Canadian Prime Minister Mackenzie King had established the Permanent Joint Board on Defense. In mid-1941, the nations tacitly approved joint defense plan ABC-22, obligating both governments to provide military forces "to their utmost capacity" to defend either from attack. Additionally, the Americans repeatedly urged full US strategic command over British Columbia, which the Canadians ultimately dismissed on January 20, 1942. The joint Pacific Coast war effort therefore remained "coordination by mutual cooperation."

Rear Admiral Robert "Fuzzy" Theobald possessed "one of the best brains and worst dispositions in the Navy" according to USN historian Samuel Morison. Theobald ranks among the worst US commanders of World War II and was forced into retirement in 1944; his own autobiography never mentions his Alaskan command. Theobald's widely discredited 1954 book *The Final Secret of Pearl Harbor* remains the de facto bible for Pearl Harbor conspiracy theorists. (Naval History and Heritage Command)

Congress had appointed Alaska Territory's civilian **Governor Ernest Gruening** in 1939. A conscientious yet pragmatic Democrat, Gruening served until 1953, then represented Alaska in the US Senate between 1959 and 1969. Alaska fell under **Lieutenant-General John L. DeWitt**'s Western Defense Command, headquartered in San Francisco's Presidio. Fiery **Major-General Simon Bolivar Buckner, Jr** commanded DeWitt's subsidiary Alaska Defense Command from Anchorage's

Fort Richardson. Buckner had forged himself into an expert on Alaskan geography and climate and was the primary reason Alaska had any preparedness to repel a Japanese offensive. Son of the eponymous Confederate lieutenant-general, the bureaucracy-despising Buckner wielded volcanic energy and proved equally gifted bellowing orders or stinging others into action via his searing wit. Buckner boasted excellent lieutenants in intelligence officer **Colonel Lawrence Castner** and senior engineer **Colonel William Talley**, who masterminded the campaign's rapidly built forward airfields.

Rear Admiral Thomas C. Kinkaid commanded cruisers or carriers during the 1942 battles of Coral Sea, Midway, the Eastern Solomons, and Santa Cruz. After the Aleutians, Kinkaid commanded the US 7th Fleet during October 1944's Battle of Leyte Gulf. Kinkaid's wartime service was distinguished by a simple, aggressive style, his easy rapport with other services, and plenty of combat. (Photo by Dmitri Kessel/ The LIFE Picture Collection/ Getty Images)

On March 8, 1942, the USAAF named cautious, methodical **Brigadier-General William O. Butler** Eleventh Air Force commander. Butler, a former US Army balloon pilot, lacked Alaska experience. Buckner effectively bypassed Butler via XI Bomber Command's **Colonel William O. "Eric" Eareckson**. Irreverent and relentless, Eareckson proved an enormously talented and innovative combat pilot who always led by example. Adored by his men, "Wild Bill" quickly became Buckner's favorite officer. Fearless but never reckless, Eareckson essentially made the Aleutian campaign his own personal war.

US Army and US Navy commands remained autonomous, with parallel, redundant command chains; their respective Anchorage and Kodiak headquarters were 400 miles apart. Interservice disputes were clunkily settled by the Joint Chiefs of Staff (JCS). Intellectual but prickly **Rear Admiral Robert A. "Fuzzy" Theobald** commanded the naval North Pacific Area; Theobald's assigned air and naval assets were designated Task Force 8. Ambitious, aggressive, and elitist **Captain Leslie E. Gehres** (USN) commanded Alaska's Patrol Wing Four (PatWing-4). Gehres is largely remembered as USS *Franklin*'s controversial skipper during that carrier's horrific March 19, 1945 inferno off Japan.

Alaskan theater difficulties would inspire several US command changes. Aggressive, battle-tested **Rear Admiral Thomas C. Kinkaid** relieved Theobald on January 4, 1943. Although not deeply intellectual, Kinkaid commanded decisively and cooperated well with Buckner. Kinkaid subordinate **Rear Admiral Charles "Soc" McMorris** would lead the cruiser–destroyer Task Group 16.6 at the March 26, 1943 Battle of the Komandorski Islands.

Alaska outsider **Major-General Albert Brown** opened the difficult May 1943 Attu battle as US Landing Force Attu commander. Kinkaid replaced Brown with Alaska veteran **Brigadier-General Eugene Landrum** just as the battle was turning. As Commander Amphibious Force, Pacific Fleet, **Rear Admiral Francis Rockwell** led Attu's invasion fleet, Task Force 51.

Highly competent **Admiral Chester W. Nimitz** commanded the US Pacific Fleet and the geographical Pacific Ocean Areas. Nimitz, however, failed to better address an explicit Alaskan chain-of-command. When pressed by Theobald, Nimitz demurred, "The command relationship between ... Alaska Defense Command under General Buckner and the Northern Pacific Force is to be by mutual cooperation."

The United States mysteriously triggered ABC-22 on May 21, 1942, claiming an Alaska invasion to be imminent and demanding Canadian reinforcements that would be reluctantly given. Canada's Pacific theater forces were commanded by **Major-General George Pearkes** of the Canadian Army's Pacific Command and **Air Vice-Marshall Leigh Stevenson** of RCAF Western Air Command.

OPPOSING FORCES

JAPANESE

The Imperial General Headquarters' Aleutian campaign intended to pre-empt a potential US offensive against Japan's North Pacific empire. Defending the Home Islands were the General Defense Command's four divisions and 11 mixed brigades, along with the IJAAF's 1st Air Army (Kokugun) of 90 aircraft. Based at the Kurile Islands were 18 Imperial Japanese Army Air Force (IJAAF) fighters at Kashiwabara, and 36 A6M2 Zero fighters and 36 G4M Betty bombers at Paramushiro.

Operation AL

Hosogaya's main strike fleet was Dai-ni Kido Butai (Second Mobile Force), comprising light carriers *Ryujo* and *Junyo*, heavy cruisers *Takao* and *Maya*, and three destroyers. Six months' attrition had frayed the IJN's once-pristine carrier aviation corps. Instead of the nominal 102 aircraft, *Ryujo*'s and *Junyo*'s improvised Aleutians air groups totaled just 63 planes: 30 A6M2 Zero fighters, 18 B5N Kate torpedo bombers, and 15 D3A1 Val dive-bombers. Many of the aircrews lacked combat experience. Carriers *Zuikaku* and *Zuiho* briefly reinforced Hosogaya before all four carriers were transferred to the Solomons in August 1942.

The June 1942 Adak–Attu Occupation Force – also known as the Army North Seas Detachment (Hokkai Shitai) – comprised 1,200 troops. On October 24, 1942, this formation was reinforced to three infantry battalions (roughly 3,300 troops) and redesignated the 2nd District, North Seas Garrison (Hokkai Shubitai). Occupying Kiska was the Maizuru 3rd Special Naval Landing Force, a detachment of 550 IJN SNLF combat troops and 700 labor troops.

A Mitsubishi A6M2-N Rufe fighter of the IJN. The Rufe was simply an A6M Zero carrier fighter fitted with pontoon floats to allow operations from bays and harbors. Rufes provided fighter defense at both Kiska and Attu, but their added floats notably degraded the Zero's legendary performance. (Wikimedia Commons/Public Domain)

Kiska and Attu bases

Japanese intentions were to transform Kiska and Attu into effective air–sea outposts. IJN destroyers, seaplane tenders, fleet submarines, and midget

Japanese airmen at Attu pose for a group photo in the snow. Lacking the necessary engineering skills, and harassed by the Americans, Japanese plans to turn Attu and Kiska into truly effective airbases never materialized. This photo was captured by the Americans after the May 1943 Battle of Attu. (© CORBIS/Corbis via Getty Images)

submarines were semi-permanently based at the islands after capture. Crucially, no Japanese Aleutian airfields became operational. Japan's assigned Aleutian garrisons lacked the high engineering skills and proper heavy equipment vital for converting the rugged islands into bases for offensive airpower projection – a significant factor in the ensuing campaign. Organic Aleutian airpower comprised only performance-limited IJN seaplanes, such as Nakajima A6M2-N Rufe fighters and four-engine Kawanishi H6K Mavis flying boats. Kiska and Attu were supported by Kuriles-based Mitsubishi G4M Betty bombers.

At least 69 anti-aircraft guns were employed at Kiska, including four 120mm dual-purpose naval guns, 22 75mm M1928s, and ten Type 96 twin-barreled 25mm pom-poms. The 75mm M1928s possessed an effective ceiling of 26,000ft and could fire 15 rounds per minute. The 25mm guns' effective ceiling was 3,000ft. Employing obsolete sound detectors and mechanical directors, Japanese flak was poorly regarded by the Americans but considered "fairly accurate under 3,500ft." Marooned in isolation for 12 months, Japanese personnel on Kiska and Attu would excavate impressive underground facilities, allowing them to weather much of the American bombing.

US–CANADIAN

Alaskan wartime effort largely entailed conjuring civilization from virgin wilderness, both to evict the Japanese and also to establish a North Pacific military route to Siberia (and potentially Japan). Untamed Alaska demanded high proportions of service troops. Alaskan military infrastructure was built and maintained by combat-qualified US Army engineers and US Navy Seabees, as well as noncombat labor battalions – often all-black units from the American South. Additionally, over 100,000 US civilians would migrate to Alaska through 1945 to construct and support this massive new infrastructure.

Somewhere in the Aleutians, American aircrew pass the interminably long hours playing cribbage, their pin-up girls displayed prominently above. In the Aleutians, the joke went, "There's a girl behind every tree." Weather made actual combat sorties unpredictable; the ceaseless fog and vicious 100mph-plus blizzards typically kept US airmen grounded and bored. (PhotoQuest/Getty Images)

Alaska bases

By June 1, 1942 Alaska hosted 45,000 US Army personnel. Anchorage's Fort Richardson was the primary Army base. Alaska's defenses were anchored by a network of airfields, many constructed with the cooperation of the Civil Aeronautics Authority. Elmendorf Field was co-located at Anchorage with Fort Richardson, while Ladd Field was inland at Fairbanks. Along the southeastern panhandle were Metlakatla's Annette Island Army Airfield and Yakutat's Yakutat Army Airfield. At Cold Bay on the Alaska Peninsula were 2,500 troops of Fort Randall Army Airfield. Seventy miles west of Dutch Harbor at Umnak Island's Otter Point was the newly established and truly primitive Fort Glenn Army Air Base, hosting 4,000 troops. Additional Army posts included small garrisons at Nome, Seward, and Skagway's Chilkoot Barracks, a 19th-century Klondike Gold Rush relic. Twenty aircraft detector stations were planned throughout Alaska, but by June 1942, the Territory possessed only two land-based radar sets: an SCR-270 (mobile) at Anchorage and an SCR-271 at Kodiak.

US Army posts totaling 6,000 troops garrisoned the three US Naval Air Stations ringing the Gulf of Alaska: Fort Mears at NAS Dutch Harbor, Fort Greely at NAS Kodiak, and Fort Ray, a coastal defense battery at NAS Sitka. They were augmented by small US Marine detachments. The nearest major USN base was at Bremerton in Washington state's Puget Sound.

US Army

The first Regular US Army unit to arrive in Alaska was the 4th Infantry Regiment. Regular Army and National Guard Coast Artillery regiments (including anti-aircraft units) also reinforced strategic locations. The campaign's largest ground formation was the California-trained US 7th Infantry Division, assigned to retake Attu and Kiska and comprising mostly National Guard members from the sunny American southwest. They would be haunted at Attu by severe logistical foul-ups. Planned for Scandinavia but debuting at Kiska were 1,400 highly trained Americans and Canadians of the joint First Special Service Force, a mountain commando brigade.

Native Alaska combat outfits included the Alaska National Guard's federalized 297th Infantry Regiment, the three volunteer militia regiments of the 6,000-strong Alaska Territorial Guard, and the platoon-sized Alaska Scouts, an elite reconnaissance team of white and indigenous outdoorsmen ultimately nicknamed "Castner's Cutthroats."

USAAF

Alaska's total USAAF strength on June 3, 1942 was 95 fighters and 46 bombers, although many aircraft were obsolete or not yet operational.

Alaskan society had been a flying culture since the 1920s; a generation of civilian bush pilots accordingly possessed deep working knowledge of Alaska's imposing geography, weather, and uniquely demanding flying skills. Buckner ensured that USAAF pilots from the mainland were well trained in-theater by a cadre of Alaskan experts; a Japanese combat pilot later claimed he "respected greatly that the Americans flew and attacked in weather which the Japanese considered impossible."

Outdated P-36 Hawk fighters were replaced in 1942 by obsolescent P-39 Airacobras and P-40 Warhawks – incidentally quite sufficient for conducting close air support and dogfighting performance-challenged A6M2-N Rufes. June 1942 saw the arrival of the first long-ranged P-38 Lightnings.

Alaska's first bombers, obsolete B-18 Bolos (militarized DC-2 airliners), were phased out through 1942 by modern B-17 Flying Fortresses, B-24 Liberators, B-25 Mitchells, and B-26 Marauders. In May 1942, two radar-equipped LB-30s (Lend-Lease model B-24s) and two radar-equipped B-17Bs from Fairbanks' Cold Weather Laboratory arrived, followed by seven more radar-equipped B-17s transferred to Elmendorf that just missed initial hostilities.

US Navy/Coast Guard

The US Coast Guard (USCG) boasted a long Alaskan presence, having policed illegal fishing in northern waters for decades. The ragtag Alaskan Navy's flagship was the modern 2,000-ton Erie-class gunboat USS *Charleston*, whose four 6in. guns "contributed about half the weight of broadside available" in spring 1942. Remaining units were eight World War I-era "four-piper" destroyers, six ancient S-class submarines, five USCG cutters, and sundry YP (Yard Patrol) boats – commandeered fishing boats. Convoys from the US mainland commenced in 1940. US Navy seaplane tenders USS *Casco*, *Gillis*, and *Williamson* forward-supported Gehres' PatWing-4 of 20 PBY Catalinas. May 1942 brought Theobald's North Pacific Force of five cruisers and four destroyers.

Naval assets transferred through low-priority Alaska as circumstances dictated. Few truly modern warships were ever assigned. US naval strength peaked during the 1943 reconquests of Attu and Kiska, headlined by auxiliary (escort) carrier USS *Nassau* and several antiquated battleships.

Canadian

Internal politics and US-Canadian relations inspired Mackenzie King's Canadian government to provide Alaska modest but valuable reinforcements. The Royal Canadian Navy (RCN) escorted Alaska-bound convoys to Anchorage and eventually the Aleutians. Based at British Columbia's Esquimalt and Prince Rupert, Canada's West Coast flotilla eventually included auxiliary cruisers HMCS *Prince Robert*, *Prince Henry*, and *Prince David*, seven corvettes, and numerous smaller vessels.

In April 1942, the Royal Canadian Air Force (RCAF) deployed the provisional Y-Wing to Alaska's Annette Island and assumed maritime patrols. X-Wing arrived at Anchorage on June 2, 1942. X-Wing comprised Bristol Bolingbrokes of No. 8 (Bomber-Reconnaissance) Squadron and P-40 Warhawks/Kittyhawks of No. 14 and No. 111 (Fighter) squadrons.

For the August 1943 liberation of Kiska, the Canadian Army provided the 5,500-strong Greenlight Force comprising the 13th Infantry Brigade

Lockheed P-38 Lightnings of the 54th Fighter Squadron, 343rd Fighter Group flying over the Aleutians, in the summer of 1943. On August 17, 1942, guided by a radar-equipped B-17, two 54th Fighter Squadron P-38s ambushed a pair of H6K Mavis floatplanes in the first use of Colonel Eric Eareckson's air-to-air radar intercept tactics. (Photo by Dmitri Kessel/The LIFE Picture Collection/Getty Images)

Group (6th Canadian Division), intentionally diverse with volunteers, Francophones, and North America-bound "zombies" (conscripts). Greenlight Force maintained its British-style organization but was fed, clothed, and equipped by the existing American logistic network.

ORDERS OF BATTLE, JUNE 3, 1942

Hull classifications:

AC	collier
AM	minesweeper
AO	oiler
AP	transport
AVD	seaplane tender destroyer
AVP	seaplane tender
BB	battleship
CA	heavy cruiser
CL	light cruiser
CV	fleet aircraft carrier
CVL	light aircraft carrier
DD	destroyer
M	minelayer
PG	patrol gunboat
SS	submarine
USCGC	US Coast Guard cutter
YP	patrol craft

JAPANESE

NORTHERN FORCE, FIFTH FLEET (IJN) – VICE ADMIRAL BOSHIRO HOSOGAYA

Second Mobile Force (Dai-ni Kido Butai) – Rear Admiral Kakuji Kakuta
Carrier Group (Carrier Division 4)
CVL *Ryujo* (flagship) (12 x A6M2, 18 x B5N1/B5N2)
CV *Junyo* (18 x A6M2, 15 x D3A1)

Support Group
Cruiser Division 4
- CA *Maya*
- CA *Takao*

Destroyer Division 7
- DD *Akebono, Ushio, Sazanami*
- AO *Teiyo Maru*

Main Body – Vice Admiral Boshiro Hosogaya
CA *Nachi* (flagship)
DD *Inazuma, Ikazuchi*
Supply Group
- AO *Fujisan Maru, Nissan Maru*
- 3 x cargo ships

Kiska Invasion Force – Captain Takeji Ono
Cruiser Division 21
CL *Kiso*
CL *Tama*
Auxiliary cruisers *Asaka Maru, Awata Maru*
Destroyer Division 6
DD *Hibiki, Akatsuki, Hokaze*
AP *Hakusan Maru* (IJN Maizuru 3rd SNLF – 550 troops)
AP *Kumagawa Maru* (IJN Maizuru 3rd SNLF – 700 labor troops, construction equipment)
Minesweeper Division 13
AM *Hakuho Maru, Kaiho Maru, Shinkotsu Maru*
Attu-Adak Invasion Force – Rear Admiral Sentaro Omori
CL *Abukuma*
Destroyer Division 21
DD *Wakaha, Nenohi, Hatsuharu, Hatsushimo*
M *Magane Maru*
AP *Kinugasa Maru* (IJA 301st Independent Infantry Battalion – 1,200 troops)

GUARD FORCE (IJN) – VICE ADMIRAL SHIRO TAKASU

Battleship Division 1
BB *Hyuga* (flagship)
BB *Ise*
BB *Fuso*
BB *Yamashiro*
Cruiser Division 9
CL *Kitakami*
CL *Oi*
Destroyer Division 20
DD *Asagiri, Yugiri, Shirakumo, Amagiri*
Destroyer Division 24
DD *Umikaze, Yamakaze, Kawakaze, Suzukaze*
Destroyer Division 27
DD *Ariake, Yugure, Shigure, Shiratsuyu*

UNITED STATES

ALASKA DEFENSE COMMAND (US ARMY) – MAJOR-GENERAL SIMON BOLIVAR BUCKNER, JR

Fort Richardson (Anchorage)
4th Infantry Regiment
75th Coast Artillery (AA) Regiment
1st Battalion, 297th Infantry Regiment
Company B, 194th Tank Battalion
Alaska Defense Command Scout Detachment (Provisional)
Fort Greely (Kodiak)
201st Infantry Regiment
1st Battalion, 1st Infantry Regiment
215th Coast Artillery (AA) Regiment
Detachment 50th Coast Artillery Regiment
Detachment 250th Coast Artillery Regiment
2nd Battalion, 30th Field Artillery Regiment
Fort Mears (Dutch Harbor)
37th Infantry Regiment
206th Coast Artillery (AA) Regiment
Detachment 250th Coast Artillery Regiment
Fort Glenn (Umnak)
2nd Battalion, 153rd Infantry Regiment
807th Engineer Aviation Battalion
Fort Raymond (Seward)
Detachment 3rd Battalion, 153rd Infantry Regiment
Marks Army Airfield (Nome)
Detachment 3rd Battalion, 153rd Infantry Regiment
Yakutat Army Airfield (Yakutat)
Detachment 3rd Battalion, 153rd Infantry Regiment
Annette Island Army Airfield (Metlakatla)
1st Battalion, 153rd Infantry Regiment
Fort Ray (Sitka)
Detachment 250th Coast Artillery Regiment

TASK FORCE 8 (US NAVY) – REAR ADMIRAL ROBERT "FUZZY" THEOBALD

North Pacific Force (TG 8.6) – Theobald
CA *Indianapolis*
CA *Louisville*
CL *Nashville* (flagship)
CL *Honolulu*
CL *St Louis*
Destroyer Division 11 – Commander Frederick Moosbrugger
DD *McCall, Gridley, Humphreys, Gilmer*
Destroyer Striking Group (TG 8.4)
DD *Case, Reid, Sands, King, Kane, Brooks, Dent, Waters, Talbot*
Surface Search Group (TG 8.2) – Captain Ralph C. Parker
PG *Charleston* (flagship)
AM *Oriole*
USCGC *Haida, Onondaga, Cyane, Aurora, Bonham* (US Coast Guard)
15 x YP boats (Commander Charles "Squeaky" Anderson)
Tanker Group (TG 8.9)
AO *Sabine, Brazos*
Steam ship *Comet* (civilian)
Submarine Group (TG 8.5) – Commander Burton G. Lakes
SS *S-18, S-23, S-27, S-28, S-34, S-35*
Air Search Group (TG 8.1) – Captain Leslie E. Gehres
Patrol Wing 4
VP-41 (10 x PBY-5A)
VP-42 (10 x PBY-5A)
AVP *Casco*
AVD *Gillis, Williamson*

AIR STRIKING GROUP (TG 8.3) (USAAF ELEVENTH AIR FORCE) – BRIGADIER-GENERAL WILLIAM BUTLER

Fort Randall Army Airfield (Cold Bay)
Detachment 11th Fighter Squadron (12 x P-40E)
Detachment 12th Fighter Squadron (12 x P-40E)
Detachment 73rd Bombardment Squadron (Medium)/28th Composite Bombardment Group (6 x B-26A)
Fort Glenn Army Air Base (Umnak)
11th Fighter Squadron (12 x P-40E)
Detachment 77th Bombardment Squadron (Medium)/28th Composite Bombardment Group (6 x B-26A)
1 x B-17B
Naval Air Station Kodiak
12th Fighter Squadron (17 x P-40E)
Detachment 18th Fighter Squadron (5 x P-36A)
Detachment 42nd Fighter Squadron/54th Fighter Group (3 x P-39D)
Detachments 36th Bombardment Squadron (Heavy)/28th Composite Bombardment Group (3 x B-18A, 2 x LB-30, 1 x B-17E)
Elmendorf Field (Anchorage)
28th Composite Group – Lieutenant-Colonel William O. Eareckson
73rd Bombardment Squadron (Medium) (5 x B-26A)
77th Bombardment Squadron (Medium) (6 x B-26A)
36th Bombardment Squadron (Heavy) (9 x B-18A, 7 x B-17E)
Provisional XI Interceptor Command – Colonel Norman D. Sillin
18th Fighter Squadron (3 x P-36A, 2 x P-40E)
54th Fighter Squadron/55th Fighter Group (24 x P-38E)
54th Fighter Group (5 x P-39D)

OPPOSING PLANS

JAPANESE

Early 1942 found Yamamoto obsessed with destroying the US Pacific Fleet before American industrial power made Japan's war unwinnable. To lure the Americans, Yamamoto conceived Operation *MI*: the capture of the Hawaiian atoll of Midway, presumably leading to the US carriers' destruction when they responded to the invasion.

Naval GHQ preferred its own Operation *FS*, a plan to isolate Australia by invading Fiji and Samoa, and already ratified by the IJA. Between April 2 and 5, 1942, at a heated IJN conference in Tokyo, staff officers from Naval GHQ "logically dismembered" Combined Fleet officers' competing *MI*, but a telephone call to Yamamoto cowed Naval GHQ into accepting the Midway plan on April 5. However, Naval GHQ insisted Yamamoto combine Operation *MI* with its own Operation *AL*, which would "capture or demolish [US outposts in the] western Aleutian Islands ... to check the enemy's air and ship maneuvers in this area." Aleutian-based air and sea patrols, combined with those from Midway 1,000 miles south, "would provide a perfect shielding opportunity for Japan" while the Aleutians would "protect ... Midway from a possible attack from the north." Initially the IJA rejected *MI* and *AL*, but the April 18 Doolittle Raid shocked the IJA into approving Yamamoto's plan on April 20.

Until 2005, Western narratives invariably portrayed Operation *AL* as a Japanese feint to lure US carriers from Midway. This notion had always been implausible for practical reasons of time and space: Dutch Harbor is 2,290 miles from Pearl Harbor – 4–5 days' steaming time by carrier task force. Yet Yamamoto scheduled simultaneous opening attacks for Dutch Harbor and Midway – June 3. On May 26, Nagumo's Kido Butai suffered a 24-hour sailing delay, postponing the initial Midway attack to June 4 – still insufficient lead time for a diversion. Additionally, Yamamoto's submarine screen, tasked with reporting US carrier movements, assembled to the west between Pearl Harbor and Midway, not to the north between Hawaii and Alaska. Finally, no Japanese sources actually claim *AL* was a diversion.

The Midway invasion would occur on N-Day, June 6. Almost the entire IJN Combined Fleet would sortie for the Midway–Aleutians operation, with formations scattered almost uselessly across the Central and Northern Pacific "as if Yamamoto was trying to find something for them to do." The entire plan's success rested on Kido Butai's four fleet carriers *Akagi*, *Kaga*, *Soryu*, and *Hiryu* first eliminating Midway's airpower, then destroying any US carriers that appeared. Lurking 300 miles west of Vice Admiral Chuichi Nagumo's Kido Butai was *MI*'s powerful Main Body, where Yamamoto would personally oversee the US Pacific Fleet's deathblow from his flagship, superbattleship *Yamato*.

Battle would open June 3. Hosogaya's Northern Force would pre-emptively strike Alaska's Dutch Harbor with light carriers *Ryujo* and *Junyo*, then invade the Aleutian islands of Adak and Kiska (Operation *AOB*) on June 6. After destroying an assumed US Marine base, Japanese troops would evacuate Adak and invade Attu (Operation *AQ*), with all operations complete by June 12. Once captured, Kiska and Attu would host the Base Force, consisting of aircraft assigned from the IJN's Eleventh Air Fleet. Vice Admiral Shiro Takasu's Guard Force, comprising battleships *Ise*, *Hyuga*, *Fuso*, and *Yamashiro*, two light cruisers, and 12 destroyers, would position itself 500 miles south of Kiska and 500 miles north of Midway as distant cover to either Hosogaya or Yamamoto "if events warranted."

Vice Admiral Boshiro Hosogaya's wartime service as IJN Fifth Fleet commander was marked by consistently passive conduct, both strategically and tactically. Hosogaya was cashiered on March 28, 1943. His replacement Vice Admiral Shiro Kawase fared little better. (Naval History and Heritage Command)

On May 20, Yamamoto's Northern Naval Force Order No. 24 outlined a highly choreographed "naval ballet" of three successive Aleutian Distributions. Yamamoto's First Distribution would open June 3 as stated. Once Kiska and Attu were secure, the Second Distribution would dissolve the two naval invasion forces and transfer most units into Hosogaya's Main Body in "support of the entire Aleutian Operation," while seven more I-type submarines would augment the six already present in Alaskan waters. From Midway, Kakuta's Dai-ni Kido Butai would be joined by light carrier *Zuiho* and four destroyers.

On June 20, the Third Distribution would finalize Hosogaya's force for long-term North Pacific defense. Major surface reinforcements would include battleships *Hiei* and *Kirishima* and heavy cruisers *Myoko* and *Haguro*. From Japan, fleet carrier *Zuikaku* would reinforce Kakuta's Dai-ni Kido Butai, which would divide into the First and Second Raiding Groups of two carriers each. A total of 80 Japanese warships were to parade through the Aleutian theater by June 20, including eight battleships. In these few weeks the Combined Fleet expected to burn more fuel and steam more miles than in any previous year.

Japanese intelligence on Alaska was almost non-existent, despite Japanese fishing trawlers plying Alaskan waters for decades. By early 1942, Japan's 8–10 Alaskan spies had been silenced by the internment of the Territory's 230 Japanese-Americans. Additionally, suspicious Nordic supremacist literature provoked Colonel Lawrence Castner, Buckner's intelligence officer, to root out an Alaskan Nazi-sympathizer spy ring directed from Tokyo by Hauptmann Fritz Wiedemann. Virtually all Axis intelligence on Alaska thus ended.

UNITED STATES

American armchair strategists anxiously fantasized Alaska as a Japanese springboard to invade the US mainland. However, US military professionals believed Alaska impregnable to deep overland invasion. The undeveloped territory was too vast, its arctic climate and mountainous terrain too hostile.

The IJN's four-engined Kawanishi H6K Mavis flying boat patrol bomber is seen here. The Mavis was an example of the IJN's ability to innovate technological solutions to problems. However, small numbers and the Aleutians' heavy weather conditions rendered the Mavis much less effective in-theater than the IJN had hoped. (World War II Database)

Buckner quipped, "If the Japanese come, they may get a foothold. But it will be their children who get as far as Anchorage, and their grandchildren who'll make it to the States. And by then they'll all be American citizens anyway!" Nevertheless, Alaska was still American home territory populated by US civilians – a Japanese landing on the Alaska mainland loomed as a political fiasco.

Alaska's long, rugged coastline was mostly vulnerable to air raids and amphibious lodgments capable of staging further air–sea operations. Buckner understood that garrisoning Alaska's handful of significant settlements, ports, and bases effectively defended the entire territory. However, any intelligence on Japanese plans would greatly assist Alaska's defense.

The US Navy's cryptological outfit OP-20-G had labored since early 1942 to crack JN-25B, the IJN's main operational-level code. Japanese administrative failures delayed JN-25B's scheduled changeover to JN-25C from April 1 to May 1, then May 27. The delay proved fatal. OP-20-G achieved its major breakthrough in April 1942, allowing it to break 85 percent of Japanese JN-25B signals. Yet considerable guesswork was still required, much of it done by Hawaii's HYPO station, commanded by the brilliant Lieutenant-Commander Joseph Rochefort. On April 27, HYPO intercepted a Japanese query of US air strength at "AOE" and "KCN," identified as Dutch Harbor and Kodiak, while joint US–Australian naval intelligence in Melbourne translated a message from IJN Second Fleet's Admiral Nobutake Kondo requesting charts of the Gulf of Alaska. After careful analysis, Nimitz's chief intelligence officer, Lieutenant-Commander Edwin T. Layton, warned of a possible Japanese Aleutians offensive "in late May," while on May 13, HYPO translated an unidentified IJN transmission requesting a nautical chart of Anchorage waters.

Meanwhile, HYPO was also cracking the interconnected Operation *MI*, most famously through the ingenious Midway water distillation ruse. Less dramatically, by May 15,

Appropriately dressed US personnel struggle to extricate a PBY-5A Catalina from frozen Kodiak Bay, winter 1942–43. Gehres' US Navy patrol wing no doubt agreed with the official USAAF history: "Each theater tended to think of its weather as the worst, but certainly none had a more just claim to that dubious honor than Alaska." (World War II Database)

A US cruiser and transport flank a supply-jammed Kodiak pier in *Fighter and Freighter*, a 1942 oil painting by William Draper. The American cultural genius for logistics eventually proved an overwhelming advantage, but it wasn't perfect. Months of little more than canned Spam and Vienna sausages proved an inadequate diet; one American doctor lost all his teeth in the Aleutians due to malnutrition. (Courtesy of Navy Art Collection, Naval History and Heritage Command)

careful US cryptanalysis predicted a Japanese attack on Dutch Harbor between May 30 and June 10 and concluded it was intended as a diversion from Midway. With its 12-day range for the Dutch Harbor attack and tentative speculation of IJN motives, this initial May 15 intelligence bulletin is the likely source for the uncorrected "Aleutians-as-Midway-diversion" narrative Western historians clung to for 60 years. By May 24, HYPO had accessed the full operational orders and orders of battle for *MI* and *AL*, and on May 28, Nimitz could confidently peg the attack dates as June 3 for Dutch Harbor and June 4 for Midway.

Nimitz recognized Midway as the operational *Schwerpunkt* and the western Aleutians as comparatively worthless; he deployed his forces accordingly. Rear Admiral Frank "Jack" Fletcher's TF-17 (Task Force 17) and Rear Admiral Raymond Spruance's TF-16 would ambush Yamamoto off Midway. Fletcher's *Yorktown* and Spruance's *Enterprise* and *Hornet* comprised every available US carrier in the Pacific. Nimitz intended to leave Aleutian defense to local Alaskan forces. However, US Navy chief Ernest King's May 17 instructions to form a "North Pacific Force" prompted Nimitz to send "not much more than a token force to Alaska" comprising five cruisers and four destroyers under Rear Admiral Robert "Fuzzy" Theobald.

On May 21, the US Joint Chiefs declared a state of fleet-opposed invasion in Alaska, putting all aviation units under Theobald's command and directing Buckner to coordinate with Theobald. If the Japanese landed on Kodiak or the Alaskan mainland, a state of land-opposed invasion would be declared and the arrangement reversed. Until then, Theobald was to "be governed by the principle of calculated risk" while carrying out Nimitz's orders to "oppose the advance of the enemy in the Aleutian-Alaskan area, taking advantage of every favorable opportunity to inflict strong attrition."

THE CAMPAIGN

OPERATION *AL*, JUNE 3–11, 1942

By May 25, Vice Admiral Boshiro Hosogaya's Northern Force had assembled at northern Honshu's Ominato Naval Base. Northern Force embarked the Kiska and Attu/Adak landing forces, which had been conducting amphibious training at Mutsu Bay and Hokkaido, then sortied from Ominato at 1200hrs, May 26. Hosogaya's Main Body and both invasion flotillas would put in at Paramushiro on June 2, before departing for the western Aleutians on June 3. Kakuta's Dai-ni Kido Butai, centered around light aircraft carriers *Ryujo* and *Junyo*, would bypass Paramushiro, cruising directly from Ominato to pre-emptively strike NAS Dutch Harbor on the eastern Aleutian island of Unalaska.

Meanwhile, bound for their Midway destiny, Vice Admiral Chuichi Nagumo's *Akagi*, *Kaga*, *Soryu*, and *Hiryu* sortied from Hiroshima Bay's Hashirajima Naval Base at 0600hrs on May 27. Following 24 hours behind Nagumo was Yamamoto's Main Body, the admiral flying his flag aboard superbattleship *Yamato*. Operation *MI*'s separate invasion and support flotillas converged toward Midway via the Marianas.

Nimitz's TF-8 commander Rear Admiral "Fuzzy" Theobald arrived at Kodiak, Alaska on May 27 and opened an immediately dissonant multi-day strategy conference with Major-General Simon Bolivar Buckner (US Army), Brigadier-General William Butler (USAAF), and Captain Leslie Gehres (USN). Primitive forward airfields at Umnak and Cold Bay – consisting of tents and Marston matting laid down directly on boggy muskeg – were currently unoccupied. Overruling Butler's airstrip safety concerns, Theobald ordered all air units stationed as far forward as possible. Six P-40s of Major Jack Chennault's 11th Fighter Squadron transferred to Umnak's Fort Glenn, along with six B-26s of the 77th Bombardment Squadron (Medium). Deploying to Cold Bay's Fort Randall were 12 P-40s of the 11th and 12th Fighter squadrons and six B-26s of the 73rd Bombardment Squadron (Medium). As mainland Alaska's air units shifted forward, their stations were taken by units behind them, including the RCAF's No. 111 Fighter Squadron and No. 8 Bomber-Reconnaissance Squadron, rushed forward from Yukon Territory to Anchorage.

The following day, May 28, Nimitz forwarded Theobald a new naval intelligence assessment claiming Japanese invasion forces were divided into two groups, one bound for Kiska and the other possibly for Attu. Nimitz also forwarded an intercepted May 22 IJN communiqué stating "heavy bomber force will advance to Paramushiro for a period of about 20 days beginning

Operations *AL* and *MI*, May 26–June 11, 1942

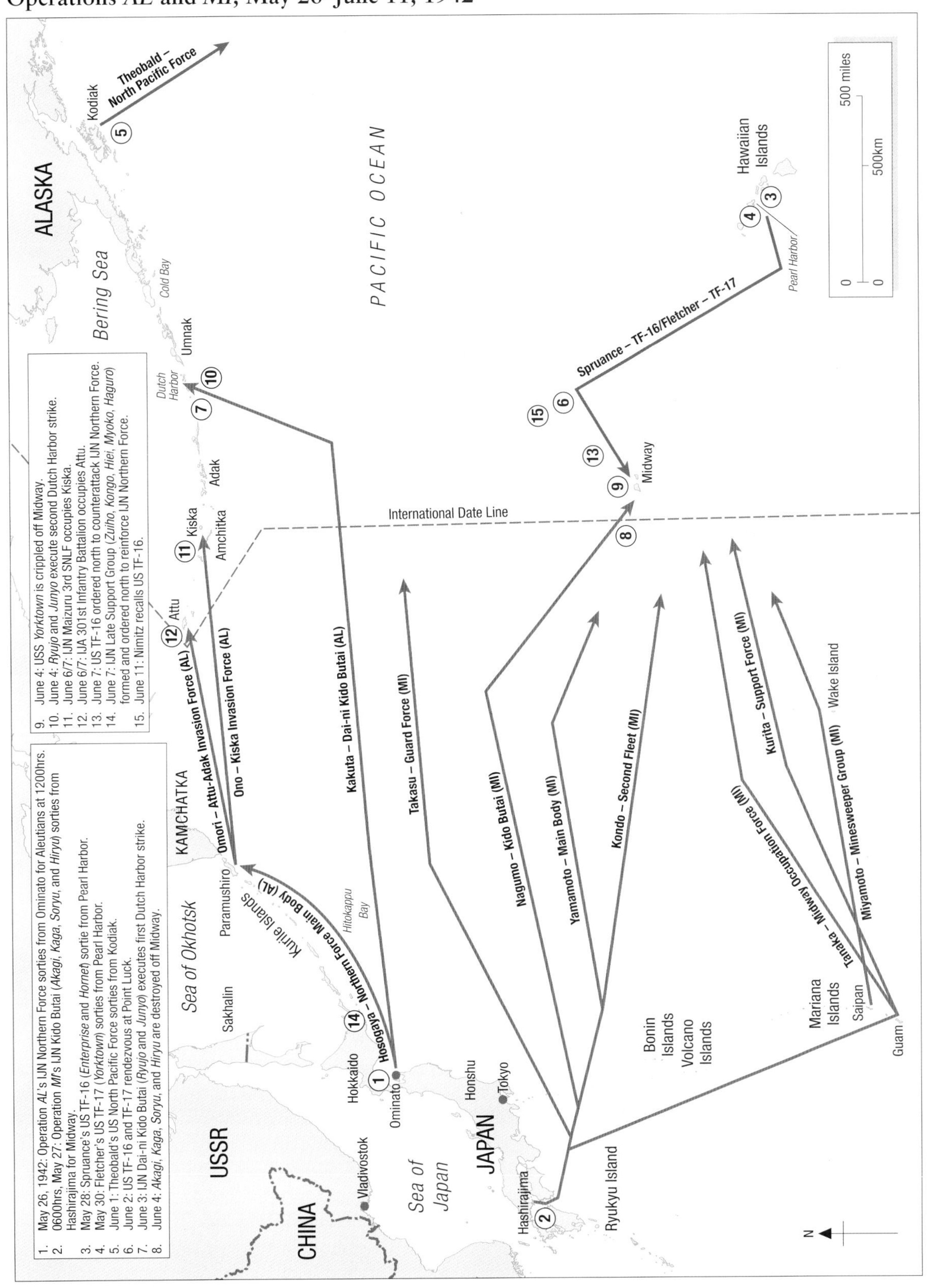

A 1934 photo of Kakuta's flagship *Ryujo*. A purpose-built, flush-decked 10,150-ton light carrier of 29 knots, she made an odd pairing with brand new *Junyo*, a 25-knot former ocean liner displacing 24,150 tons. None of the IJN light carriers proved as operationally useful as the US Navy's later Independence class. (World War II Database)

May 29." Additionally, increasingly heavy IJN anti-submarine patrols were noted in the North Pacific.

Theobald harbored a pathological suspicion of naval intelligence, reinforced by Pearl Harbor. Deigning the western Aleutians too worthless to warrant an invasion, Theobald disregarded Nimitz's premise that Kiska and Attu were the primary targets. Theobald's May 29 memo announced that Japanese transmissions were intended to lure US forces forward, leaving the true Japanese targets undefended.

Theobald therefore chose to defend Dutch Harbor and mainland Alaska. Radiating outwards from Dutch Harbor cruised naval picket lines composed of Commander Charles "Squeaky" Anderson's YP boats and Commander Burton Lakes' six S-boat submarines. The Alaskan Navy's World War I destroyers would station at Unalaska's nearby Makushin Bay as a final defense to a Dutch Harbor invasion. Theobald's cruiser–destroyer North Pacific Force would deploy far to the rear beneath land-based air cover – in the Gulf of Alaska 500 miles east of Dutch Harbor – until the Japanese carriers had been neutralized. Though a theater commander, Theobald would command at sea from light cruiser *Nashville*. Departing Kodiak on June 1, Theobald transmitted to Nimitz, "Hereafter cannot communicate without breaking radio silence from sea which I desire to avoid if possible."

Prewar Japanese intelligence on Dutch Harbor was almost non-existent, consisting of poor charts and a single 1920s photograph. However, *I-19*'s June 2 periscope reconnaissance accurately assessed Dutch Harbor's garrison at only 5,000 mostly service personnel instead of the assumed US Army division. Urged by Rear Admiral Sentaro Omori, Kakuta requested to invade Dutch Harbor instead, but the last-minute notion was too radical for Yamamoto, who refused.

The Battle of Dutch Harbor, June 3–4

Ryujo and *Junyo* approached their launch point 165 miles south of Dutch Harbor during the short summer night of June 2/3. They were masked by the region's typically thick fog, which, to Kakuta's anxiety, actually delayed local twilight. With the mercury reading 19 degrees F, *Ryujo* and *Junyo* began belatedly launching their planes at 0250hrs, eight minutes before the northern summer's local sunrise. Kakuta's 46-plane strike consisted of *Ryujo*'s 15 B5N Kates and three A6M2 Zeroes, and *Junyo*'s 15 D3A Val dive-bombers and 13 A6M2 Zeroes. A *Ryujo* Kate crashed on take-off, but its crew were promptly rescued by a destroyer.

The fog and 400ft cloud ceiling precluded formation flying; planes made their way individually to Dutch Harbor. Believing the overcast too low for effective dive-bombing, *Junyo*'s entire strike of 15 Val dive-bombers aborted, along with 11 of *Junyo*'s 13 Zeroes. Japanese knowledge of Dutch Harbor installations was so poor the pilots had been briefed simply to attack any enticing-looking target. The Japanese were unaware of US fighter strips at Umnak and Cold Harbor, believing the nearest US fighters were based 600 miles away at Kodiak.

Several Fort Mears barracks burn after being bombed by B5N Kate level bombers the early morning of June 3, 1942. The attack on the barracks killed 25 Americans – 17 from the 3rd Battalion, 37th Infantry Regiment, and eight from the 151st Combat Engineer Regiment. The 3rd Battalion, 37th Infantry Regiment had just arrived the previous evening from Seattle. (NARA via Tracy White)

Dutch Harbor's shore-based anti-aircraft defenses comprised the Arkansas National Guard's 206th Coast Artillery (Anti-Aircraft) Regiment's batteries of twelve 3in. (76.2mm) M1918 AA guns, fourteen 37mm AA guns, and twenty-four 0.50-caliber M2 Browning heavy machine guns. A coastal artillery battery of four 155mm Long Tom guns from the 250th Coast Artillery Regiment guarded the harbor approaches, but were useless against aircraft. Moored in harbor were old flush-deck destroyers USS *King* and USS *Talbot*, seaplane tender USS *Gillis*, submarine USS *S-27*, US Army transports USAT *President Fillmore* and USAT *Morlen*, and Coast Guard cutter USCGC *Onondaga*.

Dutch Harbor's 6,282-strong garrison had been waiting several days for the rumored Japanese attack and duly went to General Quarters at 0430hrs. Three days' stormy weather broke that morning, brilliantly revealing Dutch Harbor under a 10,000ft cloud ceiling. At 0540hrs, Gillis' radar detected incoming aircraft at 9,000ft. NAS Dutch Harbor skipper Commander William Updegraff observed, "Looks like this is it," and ordered an alert. Ships in port made steam to escape. Dutch Harbor broadcast, "About to be bombed by enemy planes." P-40s in Cold Bay, 180 miles east, scrambled to intercept the Japanese. Radio failure meant Chennault's P-40s at Umnak's much closer Fort Glenn were oblivious to the impending attack.

Five minutes later, at 0545hrs, the IJN planes appeared and made a strafing pass of Dutch Harbor facilities. Two Catalinas were in the midst of taking off when the Japanese attacked. Two Zeroes shot down one of the Catalinas, killing two aboard. The flaming PBY crash-landed and its pilot escaped just before it exploded. The second Catalina got airborne and fled safely into the clouds.

A torpedo-armed B-26 Marauder at a typically rough Aleutian airfield. The B-26 was a notoriously hot ship to handle, even inspiring a Congressional investigation. Called "The Flying Prostitute" and worse, the Marauder's high landing speed made it especially dangerous operating from short, rough Aleutian airstrips. (© CORBIS/Corbis via Getty Images)

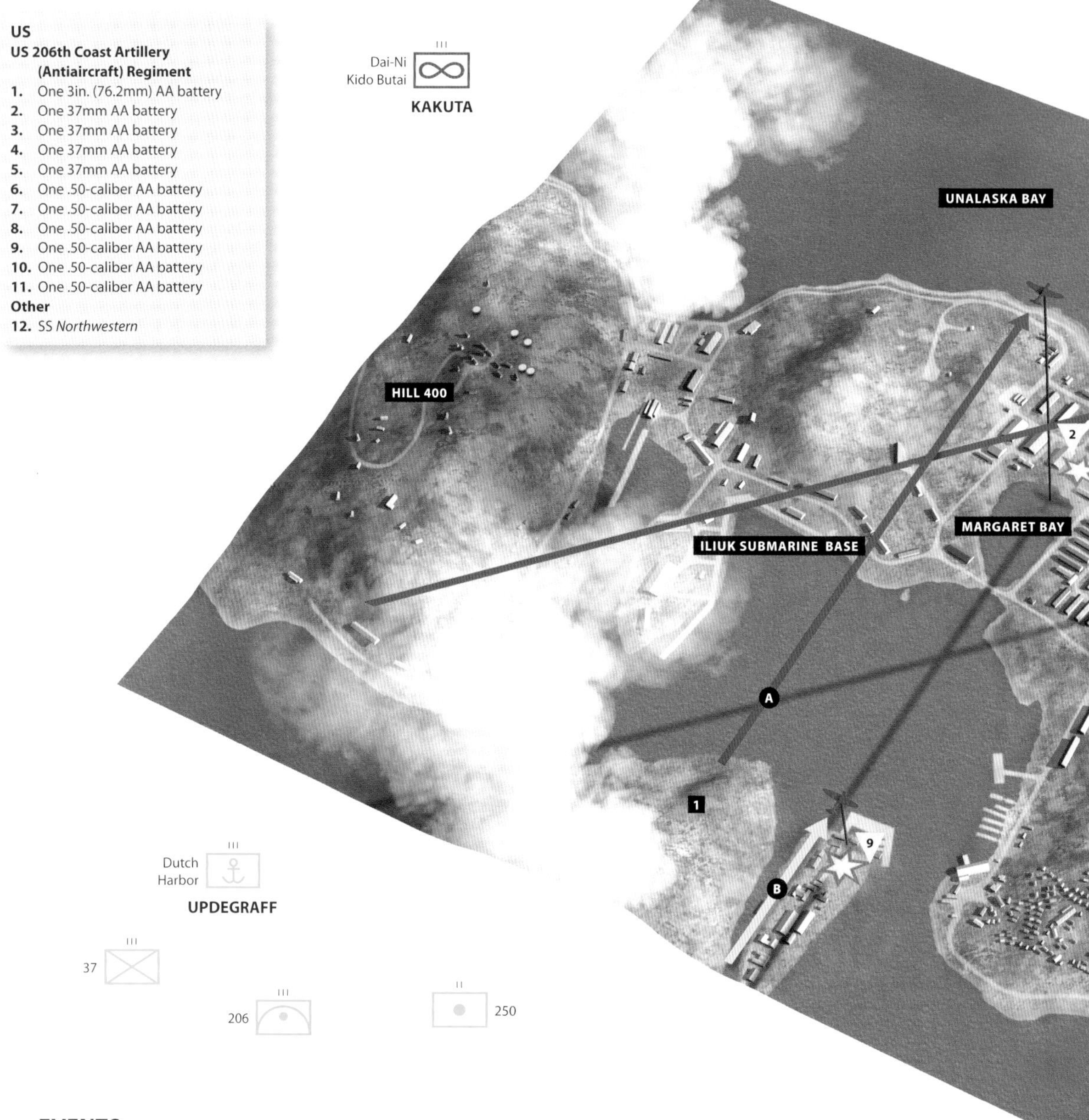

EVENTS

1. At 0545hrs, Lieutenant Hiroichi Samejima's six B5N Kates and eight A6M Zeroes strafe Dutch Harbor facilities and shoot down a PBY in the midst of take-off. One Zero is claimed shot down, shared by a PBY waist-gunner and seaplane tender USS *Gillis*.

2. Flying at 9,000ft, four Kates strike Fort Mears facilities with 14 of 16 293lb bombs dropped at 0550hrs. Three warehouses, two barracks, and three Quonset huts are destroyed and 25 Americans are killed.

3. Aiming for Fort Mears barracks, three Kates drop six 550lb bombs, missing Fort Mears but killing a US Army soldier in a trench.

4. A third flight of Kates drops six 550lb bombs, knocking out a radio transmitter, destroying a Quonset hut, and killing a civilian worker from Siems-Drake Puget Sound.

5. The final wave of Kates approaches Dutch Harbor from the east and drops six bombs at naval facilities on Power House Hill. The Japanese depart by 0635hrs.

June 4

6. Beginning at 1755hrs, five of Lieutenant Zenji Abe's D3A Vals begin executing shallow dives from 6,000ft. They drop their bombs at 1,500ft, destroying four 6,666-barrel steel fuel tanks and 22,000 barrels of fuel.

7. A single 550lb bomb from a D3A Val strikes SS *Northwestern*, starting a fire that destroys a warehouse on shore.

8. Three D3A Vals dive-bomb the Naval Air Station pier. One bomb strikes the southeast corner of the pier without exploding.

9. Perhaps mistakenly, a single Val bombs Unalaska's Bureau of Indian Affairs hospital, destroying the empty nurses' wing.

10. At 1821hrs, four of Lieutenant Masatake Yamagami's B5N Kates approach from the northeast. Aiming for the fuel tanks on Power House Hill, most of their bombs fall in the sea, but one blows a 50ft hole in the top of the seaplane hangar at the base of Mt Ballyhoo.

11. A second bomb from the same wave of Kates strikes a US 37mm AA gun, killing two US Army gunners.

12. At 1825hrs, five Kates attack the ammunition storage area on the south slope of Mt Ballyhoo. Nine bombs fall along an access road, but one bomb kills four men at a US Navy 20mm gun. The Japanese strike departs shortly afterwards.

Note: the base map covers an area of 3 × 2km

JAPANESE

- **A.** Nakajima B5N2 "Kate"
- **B.** Aichi D3A Type 99 "Val"
- **C.** A6M Zeroes (flight paths not shown)

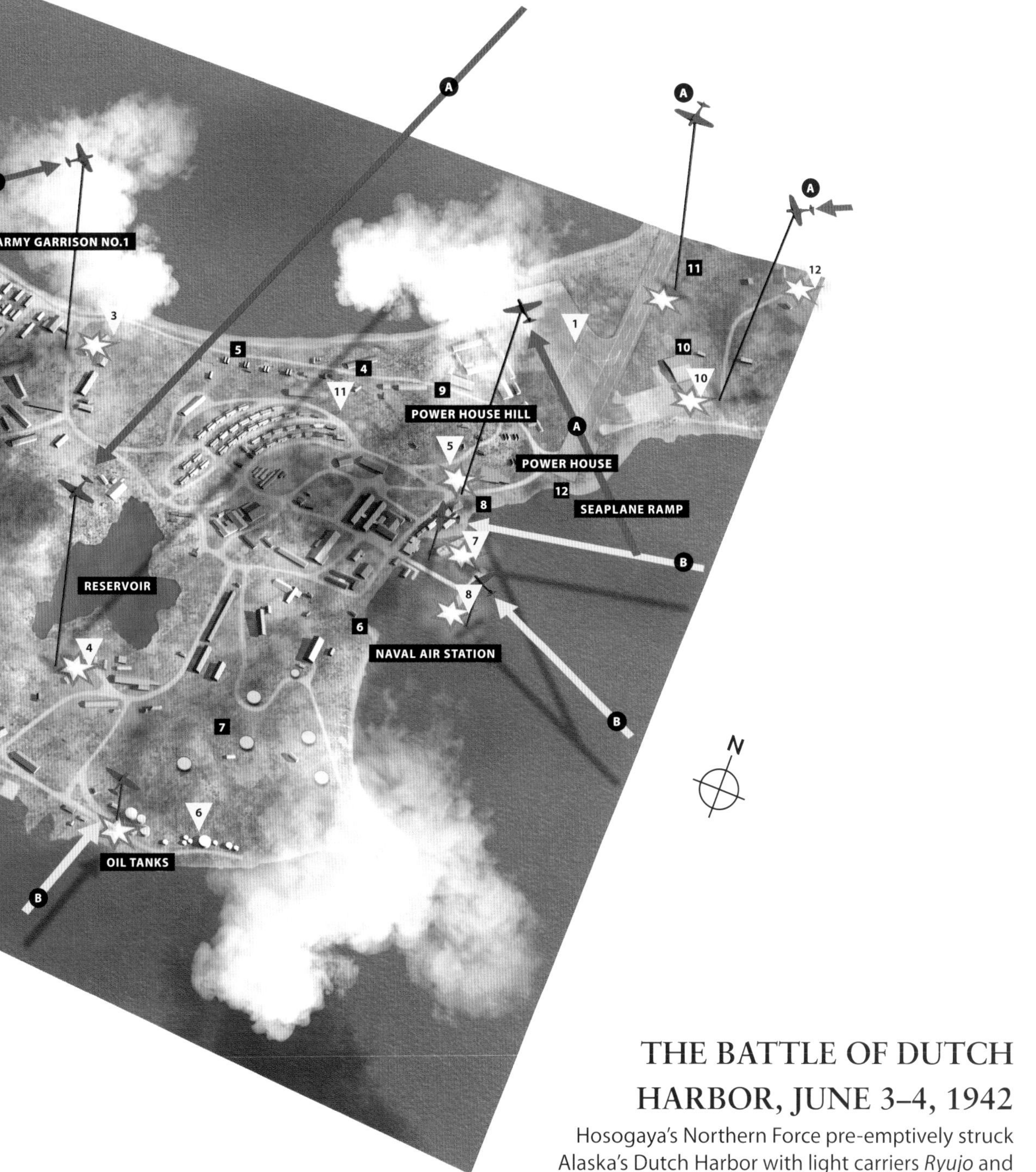

THE BATTLE OF DUTCH HARBOR, JUNE 3–4, 1942

Hosogaya's Northern Force pre-emptively struck Alaska's Dutch Harbor with light carriers *Ryujo* and *Junyo*, in preparation for the invasion of the Aleutian islands of Adak and Kiska (Operation *AOB*) on June 6.

An Aichi D3A Type 99 Val drops a 550lb bomb at Dutch Harbor, June 4, 1942. The Val's fixed landing gear gave it an archaic appearance compared to IJN and USN contemporaries. In 1942, the Val was the only IJN carrier aircraft clearly outclassed by its USN counterpart. (NARA via Tracy White)

Intense American anti-aircraft fire erupted from both shore-based artillery and ships in harbor. Commander Updegraff singled out transport *President Fillmore* for praise: "In addition to her own armament, she had mounted on deck a battery of 37mm guns consigned to Cold Bay, which gave her 22 anti-aircraft guns. These were served with such rapidity that the *Fillmore* appeared to be (and was reported) on fire." However, saddled with defective ammunition, American flak would claim just one enemy aircraft.

At 0550hrs, four Kates appeared overhead at 9,000ft. Fourteen of their sixteen 293lb bombs struck Fort Mears' teeming white installations, destroying three warehouses, two barracks, three Quonset huts, and killing 25 Americans and wounding 25 more. Three barracks, two officers' quarters, an officers' mess, and two storage sheds were damaged. Three more Kates appeared over Mt Ballyhoo and dropped six 550lb bombs, missing Fort Mears but killing an Army soldier in a trench. A third flight under Lieutenant Hiroichi Samejima dropped six more 550lb bombs, knocking out a radio transmitter, destroying a Quonset hut, and killing a civilian. The Kates' bombs narrowly missed Dutch Harbor's radio shack, spraying it with shrapnel and prompting the American yeoman to transmit, "That one knocked me off my chair!"

The final wave of Kates approached Dutch Harbor from the east and dropped six bombs on Power House Hill. One bomb hit a USN firewatcher's bunker, killing one bluejacket and wounding another. A second bomb struck a road, destroying an Army truck and killing its driver, while a third bomb landed near a trench and killed an enlisted Marine. All IJN aircraft departed Dutch Harbor to the north. Ten minutes after the Japanese disappeared, Cold Bay's P-40 Warhawks appeared over a smoke-choked Dutch Harbor. The frustrated Americans could only turn around and fly the 180 miles back to Cold Bay. No P-40s from nearby Umnak intercepted the Japanese raid on June 3.

The day's attack appeared dramatic but had inflicted only superficial damage on Dutch Harbor. The base's military value was not significantly degraded and none of Dutch Harbor's ships were damaged. Total American fatalities at NAS Dutch Harbor and Fort Mears came to 32.

Returning to *Ryujo*, an IJN pilot discovered the five flush-deck US destroyers lurking at Makushin Bay. Shortly before 0900hrs, Kakuta dispatched a 37-plane strike to find and sink the US destroyers: 15 Vals and six Zeroes from *Junyo*, six Kates and six Zeroes from *Ryujo*, and four Nakajima E8N Dave floatplanes from cruisers *Takao* and *Maya*. Quickly deteriorating weather confounded navigation and iced up the IJN planes' carburetors. Completely lost, the carrier planes returned to *Ryujo* and *Junyo*. Meanwhile, the four E8N floatplanes broke into the clear off Umnak. An 11th Fighter Squadron private on laundry duty spotted them and Chennault scrambled his P-40 Warhawks. A pair of P-40s shot down two floatplanes before the rest escaped.

At 1000hrs, a PBY was jumped by Kakuta's combat air patrol (CAP) 200 miles southwest of Dutch Harbor and shot down, killing five aircrew. Two hours later, IJN heavy cruiser *Takao* picked up three survivors, who would spend the war in Japanese captivity. A second Catalina located Kakuta's carriers and radioed their location before being shot down by Zeroes. The Catalina's crew was ultimately rescued by USCG cutter *Nemaha*; however, Dutch Harbor had not received the original transmission and *Nemaha* refused to break radio silence to relay the message.

SS Northwestern receives her single bomb hit around 1800hrs, June 4, 1942. Behind her, *President Fillmore* attempts to escape. *Northwestern* was serving as a barracks ship for civilian workers by this date. (NARA via Tracy White)

By 1200hrs, Kakuta had recovered his *Junyo* strike and the surviving Daves, shot up beyond repair. Kakuta withdrew *Ryujo* and *Junyo* southwest into stormy weather, expecting to hit Adak the following day, June 4. En route to Adak, foul weather slowed Kakuta's Dai-ni Kido Butai to nine knots. Expecting worse over Adak, and disappointed with June 3's results, the following morning Kakuta scrapped June 4's scheduled Adak strike and turned his carriers around for a second Dutch Harbor raid.

At 0900hrs, June 4, an American PBY located *Ryujo* and *Junyo* through the rainy overcast. A second Catalina radioed, "Going in to attack," but was forced to abort its brazen torpedo run on *Junyo* after Japanese fire shot out an engine.

Meanwhile, Captain Robert Meals' six B-26 Marauders took off from Umnak toward Kakuta's reported location. They were armed with air-dropped Mark 13 torpedoes, helpfully jury-rigged by USN technicians. However, Meals' B-26s were thwarted by heavy fog and cloud cover, while *Ryujo* Zeroes shot down a PBY guiding the B-26s by radar.

From Cold Bay, a frustrated Colonel "Eric" Eareckson led six more torpedo-armed B-26s out to find the Japanese; he too was rebuffed by the murk. Nevertheless, Captain George Thornbrough's B-26, having gotten lost in the storm, continued alone and found *Ryujo* and *Junyo*. Facing heavy Japanese flak, Thornbrough aborted several torpedo runs against Kakuta's violently maneuvering *Ryujo*, then changed tactics and dive-bombed his torpedo instead. The missile sailed over *Ryujo*'s heaving, storm-tossed deck and into the sea 600ft beyond. Thornbrough escaped only to fatally crash upon his next sortie.

US Marines in a Dutch Harbor trench gape as 22,000 barrels of fuel go up in smoke late on June 4, 1942. Lieutenant Zenji Abe's Vals had aborted before reaching Dutch Harbor on June 3, but struck the attack's most visible blow the following day. (World War II Database)

That afternoon, two radar-guided B-17Bs found Kakuta's fleet and attacked. Flying through intermittent fog, the lead B-17 bombed unsuccessfully from 900ft. The second B-17 bore in on heavy cruiser *Takao* and was abruptly shot down without survivors.

Meanwhile, Meals' six rearmed B-26s again departed Umnak to attack the Japanese carriers. Two B-26s dropped torpedoes at *Ryujo*, and a third B-26

Five bombs from Lieutenant Yamagami's B5N Kates, having overshot their Naval Air Station target, explode in Dutch Harbor's bay at 1821hrs, June 4, 1942. A sixth bomb blew a 50ft hole in the roof of the unfinished PBY hangar across the bay. (© CORBIS/Corbis via Getty Images)

attacked *Junyo* before escaping. Despite American claims, Kakuta's Dai-ni Kido Butai survived undamaged.

At 1600hrs, June 4, Kakuta launched his second Dutch Harbor strike, including 15 aircraft from *Ryujo* (nine B5N Kates and six A6M2 Zeroes) and 15 from *Junyo* (ten D3A1 Vals and five A6M2 Zeroes). The afternoon of June 4 brought clear skies over Dutch Harbor, with scattered clouds at 3,000ft. At 1737hrs, Fisherman's Point Army Weather Station reported a Catalina shot down near Egg Island, and at 1740hrs observed three bomber flights inbound toward Dutch Harbor.

At 1755hrs, Lieutenant Zenji Abe's Vals opened their shallow dives through the scattered overcast, releasing their 550lb bombs at 1,500ft and destroying four of Dutch Harbor's brand new 6,666-barrel steel fuel tanks. The tanks had only just been filled on June 1 from fleet oiler *Brazos* and their destruction totaled 22,000 barrels of fuel. A nearby 15,102-barrel capacity diesel fuel tank also blazed, but sturdy construction prevented it from destroying the rest of the tank farm. The Vals also attacked ancient SS *Northwestern*, a beached merchantman functioning as an auxiliary power station and civilian barracks ship for the Siems-Drake Puget Sound Company. A single bomb forward struck *Northwestern* and the ensuing blaze eventually destroyed a nearby warehouse. One Val inexplicably attacked the nearby village of Unalaska, population 250. Its 550lb bomb destroyed the empty nurses' wing of the Indian Affairs Hospital.

Four Kates followed from the northeast at 1821hrs. Most of their bombs fell in the sea, but one blew a 50ft hole in the seaplane hangar roof and another struck a US 37mm gun, killing two troops. Five more Kates attacked at 1825hrs, killing four men at a USN 20mm gun position before the Japanese departed. Ironically, the Japanese formed up for home in easy view of Fort Glenn, causing eight P-40s to scramble. A wave-top chase resulted in one Val and two P-40s shot down before the Japanese escaped.

Flight Petty Officer First Class Tadayoshi Koga's Zero streaming smoke over Dutch Harbor the evening of June 4, 1942. American anti-aircraft fire claimed few victims during the Japanese attack, but Koga was shot down by a proverbial "silver bullet" – a single .50-caliber US Navy round. (Naval History and Heritage Command)

Meanwhile, 1,800 miles to the south, Yamamoto had suffered a shocking and devastating turn of events off Midway. Just after 1020hrs on June 4, three *Yorktown* and *Enterprise* dive-bomber squadrons had abruptly destroyed Japanese carriers *Akagi*, *Kaga*, and *Soryu* in a dazzling five-minute aerial reckoning. When informed of the calamity, Yamamoto could only utter a stunned groan of despair. *Hiryu* would mortally wound Fletcher's *Yorktown* before she too succumbed to Dauntlesses that afternoon. Kido Butai was destroyed; by sunset Spruance's *Enterprise* and *Hornet* commanded air supremacy over the Central Pacific.

Billowing smoke from destroyed oil tanks roils low over Dutch Harbor the evening of June 4, 1942. The loss of 22,000 barrels of fuel was the only significant material damage done by Kakuta's June 3–4 carrier raids, but it was easily replaced by tankers. (© CORBIS/Corbis via Getty Images)

Yamamoto transmitted a message to all forces "temporarily postponing" the occupation of Midway and Kiska and tersely ordering *Ryujo* and *Junyo* south. Kakuta did not reply until he was already committed to the Dutch Harbor strike at 1530hrs, adding that a high-speed charge to Midway required his fleet to refuel. *Ryujo* and *Junyo* recovered the Dutch Harbor strike at 2026hrs, June 4 and turned toward the oiler rendezvous seven hours away. After refueling, Kakuta planned to duly depart the morning of June 5 to try and salvage Yamamoto's Midway disaster.

However, the Japanese tactical situation at Midway continued to deteriorate throughout the night of June 4/5. Finally, at 0255hrs, June 5, Yamamoto reluctantly bowed to reality, transmitting to all forces, "The Midway operation is canceled." After several attempts to lure the US carriers within gun range failed, Yamamoto ordered his surviving Midway forces to retire back to Japan.

US fatalities during the June 3–4 Dutch Harbor attacks were 43, including 33 US Army, eight US Navy, a US Marine, and a civilian. American wounded numbered 64. Twenty-five aircrew had been lost during the counterattacks, totaling 68 Americans killed or captured. Unalaska's soft muskeg had noticeably dampened the effects of near misses; besides the destruction of 22,000 barrels of fuel, little material damage had been wrought. The Eleventh Air Force had lost two B-26s, two P-40s, a B-17, and a crashed LB-30. Out of 20 PBY Catalinas, four were destroyed and two damaged, leaving 14 operational. Japanese combat losses were minimal: seven carrier planes and four floatplanes.

The US garrison assumed an invasion to be imminent; it was not immediately clear Dutch Harbor's battle was over. Theobald, increasingly agitated, had listened to radio chatter of the Dutch Harbor strikes and ineffective counterattacks throughout June 4, but was hamstrung by his self-imposed radio silence. Frustrated, Theobald temporarily handed at-sea command to *Indianapolis* skipper Captain Edward Hanson, then personally took *Nashville* back to Kodiak on June 5, arriving at 0531hrs. After further instructions to Butler, Theobald's *Nashville* departed Kodiak at 1606hrs, rejoining North Pacific Force at 0700hrs, June 6. Theobald and Gehres proceeded to waste most of their air strength scouting the empty Bering Sea, embarrassingly punctuated when five inexperienced B-17E crews mistakenly bombed the radar-detected Pribilof Islands rather than the assumed Japanese

The US Navy's 10-man Kiska weather team and two USS *Casco* personnel pose for a group photo at Kiska, late May 1942. The bluejackets' pet dog Explosion is at front and center. Third from the left in the back row is Aerographer William House. Within days all these men except House would be prisoners of the Japanese. (Naval History and Heritage Command)

fleet. Meanwhile, US reinforcements trickled forward, including 54th Fighter Squadron's P-38 Lightnings to Umnak on June 5. The USAAF additionally stripped West Coast squadrons to reinforce Alaska, dispatching six more B-24s from California and eight A-29 Hudsons and four B-17s from Edmonton, Alberta.

The invasions of Kiska and Attu, June 6/7

Despite the Midway catastrophe, at 1259hrs, June 6, Yamamoto ordered Kakuta's *Ryujo* and *Junyo* to rendezvous with Hosogaya's invasion forces and proceed with the landings at Kiska and Attu. Adak was too close to the now-revealed Umnak airbase for comfort, and the planned Adak invasion was effectively canceled.

At 2227hrs on the rainy night of June 6, the 1,260 naval infantry of IJN Commander Nifumi Mukai's Maizuru 3rd Special Naval Landing Force put ashore at Kiska's Reynard Cove and advanced southward toward Kiska Harbor. Weeks earlier, on May 18, the US Navy had established a 10-man weather station on Kiska Harbor's northwest shoreline. Visited occasionally by PBYs (and recently Buckner), the bluejackets and their pet dog Explosion were Kiska's only permanent inhabitants of the United States' westernmost outpost in the North Pacific. After burying food caches, they had nervously followed the Dutch Harbor battle by radio; they now tentatively hoped the Japanese fleet had bypassed them en route back to Japan.

At 0215hrs, June 7, the Americans were startled awake by shattering glass and Japanese 13.2mm machine-gun fire. Struck in the leg, Aerographer's Mate 2nd Class Walter Winfrey screamed, "Attack, attack!" to Aerographer's Mate 1st Class William House. Another bullet ripped through Radarman 3rd Class M.L. Courtenay's hand. The Americans frantically dressed. House and Aerographer's Mate 2nd Class J.L. Turner swiftly burned the ciphers in the stove. Two Americans were immediately captured; the remaining eight fled up the nearby mountainside, unarmed and desperate to reach the hanging cloudbank 300 yards above. Twilight was breaking. Offshore, House could make out Japanese Daihatsu barges firing up the mountain, their glowing tracers appearing "like baseballs curving toward us." Avoiding the machine-gun fire and scattering to confuse the Japanese, the

IJN Commander Nifumi Mukai's Maizuru 3rd Special Naval Landing Force lands at Kiska, June 6/7, 1942. This photo is a still from a Japanese newsreel trumpeting the Kiska invasion. The same propaganda film also featured close-ups of the recently captured US Navy weather team. (The Asahi Shimbun via Getty Images)

eight Americans reached the temporary sanctuary of the clouds but became separated in the mist. Mukai's infantry easily rooted out the buried food caches and two Americans were captured the next morning. Within days the biggest American group surrendered due to Winfrey's infected wound; operating in a beach tent, a Japanese surgeon removed the bullet lodged in Winfrey's leg. Only one American, William House, remained unaccounted for.

Some 180 miles west at Attu, Major Matsutoshi Hozumi's IJA 301st Independent Infantry Battalion landed in Holtz Bay at 0100hrs, June 7. Attu's population comprised 42 native Aleuts, including 15 children, and a white couple: 60-year-old ham radio operator Charles Foster Jones and his wife, 63-year-old schoolteacher Etta Pearl Jones. All lived in Chichagof village. No resistance was possible. The IJA battalion separated the Joneses from the Aleuts and violently interrogated them. By 0600hrs, June 8, the Jones were discovered having slashed their wrists. Charles died, but Etta recovered. On August 24, Etta Jones and the Aleuts would be confined aboard coal freighter *Osada Maru* and eventually shipped to Otaru, Hokkaido, arriving September 24. They had earned the dubious distinction of being the only American civilians captured in the United States during World War II. Of the original 44 Attuans, 24 would survive to be liberated on September 17, 1945.

Operation AL concludes

As of June 7, the Americans were still searching for Kakuta's fleet, Eareckson exhorting, "Find the bastards." Meanwhile, Kiska's and Attu's daily weather broadcasts had gone ominously silent. Far to the south, newly repaired fleet carrier USS *Saratoga* had arrived at Pearl Harbor from San Diego the previous day, June 6, before departing to rendezvous with Spruance 200 miles north of the Hawaiian island of Niihau. *Saratoga* transferred 19 Dauntlesses and 15 Avengers and Devastators to *Enterprise* and *Hornet* to replenish TF-16's Midway losses, then returned to Pearl Harbor. Nimitz then ordered Spruance north on June 8 to counterattack Kakuta. That same day, Yamamoto dispatched the Aleutians Late Support Group comprising light carrier *Zuiho*, battleships *Kongo* and *Hiei*, and heavy cruisers *Myoko* and *Haguro* to reinforce Hosogaya. From Japan, heavy carrier *Zuikaku* would also be transferred to the Aleutians as originally scheduled.

On June 8, a USAAF LB-30 reported one heavy cruiser, two light cruisers, one destroyer, and six transports in Kiska's harbor. Hours later a PBY observed a landing force at Attu. By June 10, TF-16 was halfway to the Aleutians from Hawaii, Spruance's new mission to "seek and destroy [the] enemy in Alaska." By now the airwaves were alive with Tokyo boasts that Japan had occupied Kiska and Attu. Fearing land-based airpower and sensing a trap, Nimitz recalled Spruance's *Enterprise* and *Hornet* on June 11. Despite the irritating Aleutian occupation, the United States had already won an overwhelming victory at Midway and Nimitz felt justified disengaging. The initial series of interconnected air–sea battles triggered by Yamamoto's Midway–Aleutians operation had concluded. Theobald would not finally return to Kodiak until June 13. Upon hearing Kiska and Attu had been occupied, the miserably frustrated Theobald would only be able to swear viciously.

COLONEL "ERIC" EARECKSON LEADS U.S. BOMBING RAID ON KISKA HARBOR FROM 700FT, JUNE 14, 1942 (PP. 38–39)

The first five B-24 Liberators to bomb Kiska on June 11 were from the inexperienced 21st Heavy Bombardment Squadron that had just arrived the day before. Colonel "Eric" Eareckson, the senior bomber officer and de facto bomber commander in the US Eleventh Air Force, was part of the 36th Bombardment Squadron (Heavy), equipped with B-17 Flying Fortresses. Eareckson's B-17s were down with mechanical problems, and with regret Eareckson ordered his green B-24s to Kiska, where Captain Todd's lead B-24 was shot down, losing ten men. Eareckson and his B-17s followed hours later from 3,000ft, enthusiastically claiming multiple cruiser and destroyer hits that were debunked by post-attack photographic reconnaissance.

Eareckson struck Kiska daily thereafter, adjusting his planes' bomb runs to the altitude of the day's overcast. On June 14, seen here, Eareckson leads four B-17s and three B-24s on their lowest bomb run of Kiska Harbor yet – 700ft (**1**). Numerous Japanese ships were anchored in harbor, the largest and most prestigious light cruiser *Kiso* (**2**). Japanese anti-aircraft fire erupts toward the Americans.

Japanese floatplanes, most likely F1M Petes, rose to engage. The ensuing air-to-air combat resulted in the US bombers claiming one Japanese floatplane shot down (**3**). However, available Japanese records, admittedly sparse and incomplete, do not confirm this particular air-to-air claim among their floatplanes' attrition.

Two B-17s were seriously damaged by Japanese fire. They successfully limped home to their crude field at Umnak, consisting of Marsden matting laid down directly on unstable muskeg. When landing at Umnak, US Eleventh Air Force pilots noted, fighters typically bounced 30ft and bombers drove waves into the airstrip ahead of them; Captain Russell Cone noted landing his B-17 at Umnak "felt like landing on an innerspring mattress."

Laid-back and fearless, the 42-year-old Eareckson was a former World War I infantryman and much loved by his men; during bombing missions he regularly sang to his crews to calm them. Under Eareckson's leadership, US Eleventh Air Force bombers would continue to hammer Kiska relentlessly for the next 14 months – so long as weather, ordnance, and superiors allowed. Excellent footage of several US heavy bomber runs over Kiska, captured in Technicolor, would appear in the US Army Signal Corps' 1943 film *Report from the Aleutians*, directed by John Huston.

THE LONG WINTER, JUNE 1942–MARCH 1943

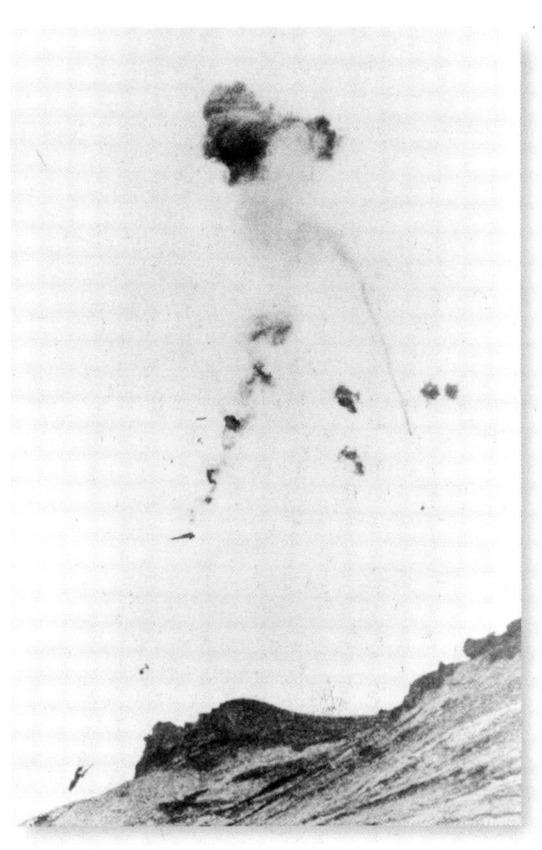

Caught on Japanese film, Captain Jack Todd's destroyed B-24 Liberator plummets toward Kiska Harbor, June 11, 1942. The exploding bomber also damaged several nearby B-24s. Gehres' PatWing-4 PBYs appeared overhead just minutes later. (The Asahi Shimbun via Getty Images)

With Kiska and Attu in Japanese hands, the next 11 months would devolve into a grim, long-range air–sea war of attrition unleashed along the full gloomy length of the Aleutian archipelago. The ensuing battles would not prove large, decisive clashes fought between powerfully arrayed forces, but an endless string of tiny, often individual life-and-death skirmishes played out across the vast loneliness of the North Pacific. Historian Brian Garfield fittingly dubbed the campaign, "The Thousand-Mile War."

Hosogaya immediately began fortifying Japan's new air–sea outposts. Under IJN Captain Sukemitsu Ito, six four-engined H6K Mavis flying boats arrived at Kiska on June 8, supplied by freighter *Kamitsu Maru*. The unpredictable weather would ultimately limit Mavis patrols to 300 miles for safety reasons. The Mavises would eventually be followed by 24 float-equipped A6M2-N Rufe fighters for air defense.

At Kodiak, Captain Leslie Gehres, commander PatWing-4, radioed Nimitz on June 10 that Kiska had been occupied, adding that Commander Norman Garton's seaplane tender USS *Gillis* was at Atka, within PBY range of Kiska. Nimitz ordered Gehres, "Bomb the enemy out of Kiska." The hard-driving Gehres unleashed a relentless round-the-clock shuttle bombing campaign forever known as "the Kiska Blitz." Though unplanned and uncoordinated, the US Navy's Kiska Blitz was simultaneous to the Eleventh Air Force's equally furious heavy bomber raids.

On the morning of June 11, five B-24 Liberators departed Cold Bay to strike Japanese shipping in Kiska Harbor from 18,000ft. Eleventh Air Force would bomb Kiska first, beating PatWing-4 by mere minutes. Over Kiska, Captain Jack Todd's lead B-24 flew into Japanese flak and abruptly exploded; the surviving B-24s dropped their bombs and turned for home. Within moments of their departure, the first of Gehres' 20 PBYs lumbered overhead. The slow, ungainly Catalina flying boats had never been intended to attack fortified targets such as Kiska; nevertheless, they dove through scattered 1,000ft overcast, strafing Japanese ships and "dropping bombs by the seaman's eye method." Japanese anti-aircraft fire damaged several PBYs, killing three, while a Catalina's near miss damaged IJN destroyer *Hibiki*. Hours later, delayed by mechanical issues, Colonel Eareckson led five 36th Bombardment Squadron (Heavy) B-17s in a bomb run against Japanese cruisers and destroyers in Kiska Harbor from below 3,000ft. Although no ships were hit, Captain Ito later recalled the June 11 attacks "came as a surprise and worried [us] considerably."

Gehres promised to keep attacking until the Japanese were expelled from Kiska or PatWing-4 expended its ordnance. For three days, PatWing-4's

Catalinas struck Kiska almost hourly. Crews quickly tired; one pilot flew 19.5 hours out of 24. *Gillis'* crew relinquished their bunks to exhausted airmen. Attrition was inevitable; Gehres' bitter aircrews sardonically nicknamed Kiska the "PBY Elimination Center." The emotionally distant Gehres, a fighter pilot who had never qualified on PBYs, later proclaimed, "Every flight was a flight that the crew should not have returned from. Every man knew this, and yet none wavered." Japanese anti-aircraft fire damaged several Catalinas beyond repair but remarkably only one Catalina was shot down over Kiska.

Inevitably, *Gillis* ran out of fuel and ordnance. After three days, seven dead, two wounded, and six Navy Crosses, the Kiska Blitz mercifully ended. Nimitz ordered *Gillis* to withdraw. After rounding up every willing native, *Gillis'* Commander Garton razed Atka's Aleut village and departed Nazan Bay at nightfall, June 13. Several Aleutian families remained behind because their men were still fishing at sea. The following day, the final Aleuts were evacuated by Garton's promised PBY; shortly afterwards, three Kiska-based H6K Mavises bombed the empty village. Hours later, a lone Catalina landed at Kanaga Island and evacuated the last USN weather team in the western Aleutians.

Meanwhile, Eareckson continued personally leading daily heavy bomber attacks against Kiska, flying beneath the fog when necessary. Six B-17s and one B-24 had struck Kiska Harbor from 1,200ft on June 12; the following day, Eareckson bombed Kiska again with five B-17s and three B-24s. On June 14, Eareckson led four B-17s and three B-24s against Kiska from below 700ft, claiming a Japanese floatplane shot down but suffering heavy damage to two B-17s. Reliant on timely, favorable weather reports and forced to bomb between occasional openings in the overcast, Eareckson's heavy bombers would be repeatedly frustrated through June. Eareckson's tactic of having a B-17 orbit Kiska and report the weather every 30 minutes proved unsuccessful. Additionally, the 1,200-mile round trip between the bombers' Umnak base and Kiska target demanded bomb-bay fuel tanks, reducing bomb loads to 3,500lb. Although bomber crews claimed numerous hits against cruisers and destroyers, little significant damage was done.

Japanese merchantman *Nissan Maru* seen burning in Kiska Harbor after being struck by Eareckson's B-17s and B-24s the morning of June 18, 1942. She would sink two hours later. Eareckson enjoyed taunting the Japanese over the radio while he was bombing them. Before long he and Tokyo Rose were regularly calling each other out by name. (Naval History and Heritage Command)

By June 15, Kiska's IJN forces afloat, commanded by Captain Takeji Ono, consisted of light cruiser *Kiso*, two destroyers, five gunboats, three sub-chasers, and several auxiliaries, including similarly named seaplane tenders *Kamikawa Maru* and *Kimikawa Maru* (and their escorting destroyers *Shokaze* and *Hokaze*), which had brought 24 floatplanes to Kiska (14 Mitsubishi F1M Petes, six Aichi E13 Jakes, and four Nakajima E8N Daves). Commander Kintaro Miura of *Kamikawa Maru* later recalled, "Personnel were highly nervous due to bombings. No great damage had been caused, but the attacks were persistent." The Japanese on Kiska moored their ships close together in harbor to concentrate their naval and shore-based anti-aircraft fire, hoping to catch US bombers as they plunged through holes in the overcast. Through June 16, Kakuta's *Ryujo*, *Junyo*, and *Zuiho* stationed 250 miles south of Kiska to intercept the US air raids, but poor weather prevented any fighter sorties.

A PBY-5A Catalina off Segula Island near Kiska, possibly during the Kiska Blitz, summer 1942. Despite its homely appearance, the Catalina proved one of the most versatile and valuable Allied aircraft of World War II. (World War II Database)

On June 18, Eareckson led five B-24s and three B-17s against Kiska from 15,000ft, losing a B-24 but sinking *Nissan Maru* and encouraging seaplane tender *Kamikawa Maru* to withdraw 90 miles west to Agattu. *Kamikawa Maru* would occasionally visit Kiska during the night or dispatch a destroyer with supplies and fuel to build the seaplane base. Eareckson's latest tactic on cloudy days was to form over Kiska Volcano and make timed dead reckoning runs at Kiska Harbor through the overcast.

On June 20, Nimitz's intelligence team interpreted two separate Bering Sea radar reports as a Japanese invasion fleet steaming for Alaska's Seward Peninsula. In addition to four IJN carriers were supposedly two battleships, five heavy cruisers, three light cruisers, 22 destroyers, and six or seven submarines. The ensuing panic inspired the first mass airlift in US history – Operation *Bingo*. Buckner seized 46 civilian aircraft and in 39 sorties lifted the first detachment of 20 anti-aircraft guns and personnel to Nome on June 21. Within two weeks, 140 more cargo planes' worth of reinforcements arrived, supplemented by merchantmen from Seward delivering additional troops, guns, ammunition, and vehicles to Nome. By early July, a Nome garrison of 2,000 US troops had been established. An additional garrison of 1,400 was established at Port Heiden on the Alaska Peninsula, eventually becoming Fort Morrow.

No Alaska landing materialized – the misinterpreted contacts had merely been Kakuta's carriers *Ryujo*, *Junyo*, and *Zuiho* fruitlessly baiting a naval confrontation. Much farther south, desultory submarine bombardments of British Columbia's Estevan Point (Commander Minoru Yokota's *I-26*) and Oregon's Fort Stevens (Lieutenant-Commander Meiji Tagami's *I-25*) on June 20–21 were ultimately judged isolated events unconnected to a greater offensive against the Pacific Northwest. By June 30, US intelligence was finally confident Kiska and Attu were the extent of Japanese ambitions in the North Pacific.

Meanwhile, on July 3, seven B-24s bombed seaplane tenders *Kamikawa Maru* and *Kimikawa Maru*, a tanker, and six destroyers at Agattu from 19,500ft. No significant damage was done, but a near miss killed and injured several aboard *Kamikawa Maru*'s bridge. Off Agattu the following day, July 4, submarine USS *Triton* torpedoed Japanese destroyer *Nenohi*. *Nenohi* capsized and sank in five minutes, killing 192 of her 228 crew. *Kamikawa Maru* was then recalled to Japan.

On June 30, a powerful resupply convoy had departed Ominato, Honshu to reinforce the Japanese outpost at Kiska. Under Hosogaya's command were carriers *Zuikaku*, *Junyo*, *Zuiho*, and *Ryujo*, protecting seaplane carrier *Chiyoda* and transport *Argentina Maru*. The 1,200 new troops would double

The Aleutian campaign, June 1942–August 1943

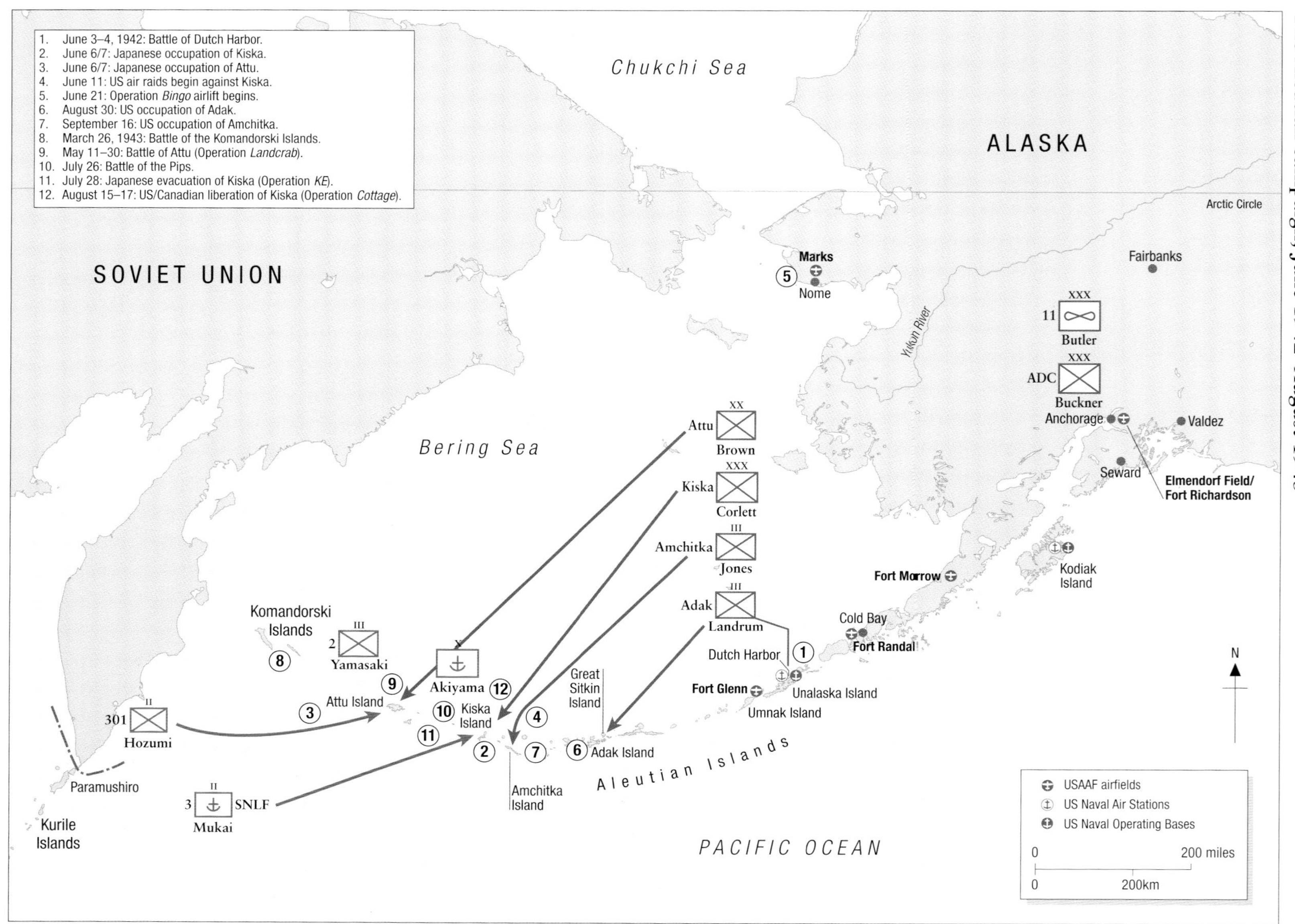

Kiska's garrison. On July 5, Hosogaya's convoy arrived at Kiska, including six midget submarines of the 5th Guard Unit, Special Purpose Unit aboard *Chiyoda*. The Japanese 12th Construction Battalion detachment began building midget submarine facilities at Kiska Harbor. Hours later, USAAF bombers attacked *Chiyoda* without result, but submarine USS *Growler* snuck into Kiska Harbor and torpedoed three Japanese destroyers, sinking *Arare* and blowing the bows off *Shiranuhi* and *Kasumi*, killing 117.

Yamamoto then withdrew carriers *Zuikaku*, *Junyo*, *Zuiho*, and *Ryujo* from the North Pacific to refit in Japan; a month later, they would be suddenly transferred to the South Pacific in response to Operation *Watchtower*, the Americans' surprise August 7 invasion of Guadalcanal. Hosogaya's chief source of air support was therefore permanently removed.

The USAAF had established the XI Bomber Command on July 1 under Colonel "Eric" Eareckson – without the customary promotion to brigadier-general. Butler explained, "Eareckson can't even spell discipline." Improvised USAAF reinforcements continued unabated, and by July 8, the desert-camouflaged B-24s of the 404th Heavy Bombardment Squadron – nicknamed "The Pink Elephants" – had begun Bering Sea patrols out of Nome.

At this point, a peculiar postscript to the June 3–4 Dutch Harbor attack suddenly emerged. During the June 4 Dutch Harbor raid, 19-year-old Flight Petty Officer First Class Tadayoshi Koga had been part of a three-ship Zero element from *Ryujo*. After Koga and his wingmen shot down a Catalina, they had strafed the survivors to death in the water. However, minutes later over Dutch Harbor an American machine-gun bullet pierced the oil line of Koga's Zero. Koga had expected to put safely down on nearby Akutan Island and wait for IJN submarines to rescue him. Upon touching down, the landing gear of Koga's Zero had immediately dug into Akutan's thick, swampy muskeg, flipping the Zero onto its back – killing Koga instantly but otherwise leaving the fighter intact.

On July 10, Koga's downed Zero was discovered from the air by one of Gehres' PBYs. After multiple failed attempts, a US ground party successfully salvaged the Zero on July 15. Transport USS *St Mihiel* would deliver the Akutan Zero to Seattle on August 1, and by September 20 the US Navy would begin comprehensively test-flying the refurbished fighter at San Diego – the first flight-worthy Zero recovered by the Allies.

The Koga Zero in its fateful Akutan bog just before salvage, July 1942. Despite popular myth, the Koga Zero did not directly inspire the F6F Hellcat. The captured fighter mostly proved useful for devising counter-tactics and for confirming that existing Allied intelligence reports on the Zero's performance were generally correct. (Naval History and Heritage Command)

Meanwhile, the North Pacific air–sea campaign continued unabated. On July 14, at the Unimak Pass chokepoint between Unimak and Akutan islands, Japanese submarine *I-7* intercepted the 2,722-ton US Army transport USAT *Arcata*, outbound from Bethel, Alaska for Seattle. *I-7* shelled and sank *Arcata*, whose crew found themselves adrift on a lifeboat for eight days. The Americans would eventually be

An American S-class submarine makes a summer departure from Dutch Harbor, *c.* 1942–43. The S-boats were so obsolete they were retired mid-war. However, they faithfully harassed the Japanese in the North Pacific in the absence of the modern fleet submarines. (Photo by Dmitri Kessel/ The LIFE Picture Collection/ Getty Images)

rescued off Kodiak Island, but only 12 of *Arcata*'s 22 crew would survive the frigid North Pacific.

The Japanese had attempted a few of their own air raids, including on July 11, when A6M2-N Rufes had futilely attacked four B-24s taking off from Umnak's Fort Glenn. The last Japanese raid was on July 20, when three of Ito's H6K Mavis bombers unsuccessfully bombed Gehres' seaplane tender *Gillis* in Adak's Kuluk Bay.

Theobald ended Eareckson's timed bombing through overcast, declaring it wasteful and ineffective; in poor weather Eleventh Air Force would instead patrol and support the US Navy's warships. Having departed Kodiak July 19, Theobald's North Pacific Force of five cruisers, five destroyers, and four destroyer-minesweepers arrived off Kiska July 21. The dense fog refused to lift and Theobald was forced to retire. A July 27 attempt was likewise canceled. In the murk, destroyer *Monaghan* and three of the destroyer-minesweepers collided but returned safely to Kodiak.

Meanwhile, on Kiska a lonely human drama drew to its inevitable conclusion. Aerographer's Mate 1st Class William House had hidden in caves by day, scoured beaches for food by night, and repeatedly evaded Japanese patrols, stray dogs, a P-38 fighter strafing, and increasingly heavy B-17 bombardments. Praying the IJN invasion was merely a raid, House had vowed to outlast the Japanese. However, one day while drinking from a creek, House had fainted from exhaustion. Recognizing impending death, House decided to surrender, writing his name on his jacket in case he was executed. Weighing 80lb, House finally emerged on July 28, telling his incredulous captors he had survived on tundra, worms, and shellfish. House casually asked if he had held out 50 days. He had. The stunned Japanese took an immediate liking to House and nursed him back to health before shipping him to Japan on September 20. House and his nine fellow weathermen would survive captivity.

Pressured by Nimitz, Theobald relinquished at-sea command of North Pacific Force to Rear Admiral William "Poco" Smith on August 3. Hours later, heavy cruisers *Indianapolis* and *Louisville*, light cruisers *Honolulu*, *St Louis*, and *Nashville*, and four destroyers again departed Kodiak for Kiska. Approaching Kiska on August 7, visibility fell to zero, but at 1934hrs, a brief hole in the fog allowed a navigational fix. At 1947hrs, North Pacific Force emerged from the fog bank and at 1955hrs, opened fire. Poor visibility, shaky navigation, and Theobald's overcautious bombardment plan compelled Smith to shell Kiska Harbor by indirect fire from a range of 11 miles. US cruisers launched six SOC Seagull floatplanes to spot shell fall. Hampered by poor visibility, the Seagulls were promptly attacked by Kiska-based A6M2-N Rufes, which shot down one Seagull, damaged three more, and scattered the rest. Meanwhile, Kiska shore batteries returned fire, an H6K Mavis bombed blindly through the overcast, and a Rufe strafed destroyer USS *Case*. At

2036hrs, Smith recovered his last surviving floatplane and retired, having expended 6,785 rounds of 8in., 6in., and 5in. ordnance.

Later analysis revealed 1,600 shell craters half a mile northeast of the apparently undamaged Japanese camp. North Pacific Force's bombardment had ravaged Kiska's muskeg, but had never threatened any great damage, prompting USAAF wits to dub the August 7 bombardment, "The Navy's Spring Plowing." Smith observed that naval bombardments were of "questionable value unless followed by the landing of troops" and suggested better results could be obtained by bombers in reasonable weather. Buckner blasted Theobald's timid bombardment plan: "He's as tender of his bottoms as a teenage girl!"

With the Guadalcanal campaign well underway, both Japan and the United States began tapping their mutual Aleutian sideshow for South Pacific reinforcements. On August 17, IJN Captain Sukemitsu Ito's three surviving Kiska-based H6K Mavis bombers transferred back to Japan. Additionally, only four of Kiska's 24 F1M Pete, E13A Jake, and E8N Dave floatplanes remained operational. Twelve had been lost to surf and weather and eight to B-17 and B-24 bombings. Meanwhile, Nimitz was forced to transfer Theobald's modern fleet submarines from Alaska to the Solomons. Left behind was USS *Grunion*, which had claimed IJN sub-chasers *SC-25* and *SC-27* off Kiska before being sunk by her own malfunctioning torpedo on July 31. Nimitz's obsolete S-boats remained to continue the US blockade.

The already strained relationship between Theobald and Buckner took a farcical nosedive on August 19. While visiting Theobald during a Kodiak staff conference, the free-spirited Buckner inexplicably recited aloud his personal "Ode to Theobald." However indiscreet, if appalling field conditions and surreal American command dysfunction distinguished the Aleutian struggle, no better paragon of the "Theater of Military Frustration" can be found:

In far Alaska's icy spray, I stand beside my binnacle
And scan the waters through the fog for fear some rocky pinnacle
Projecting from unfathomed depths may break my hull asunder
And place my name upon the list of those who made a blunder
Volcanic peaks beneath the waves are likely any morning
To smash my ships to tiny bits without the slightest warning
I dread the toll from reef and shoal that rip off keel and rudder
And send our bones to Davey Jones – the prospect makes me shudder
The Bering Sea is not for me nor my fleet headquarters
In mortal dread I look ahead in wild Aleutian waters
Where hidden reefs and williwaws and terrifying critters
Unnerve me quite with woeful fright and give me fits and jitters

Buckner claimed the jest was in good fun, but Theobald "deeply resented" the poem, especially finding its public reading "gratuitously insulting." Incensed, Theobald forwarded the doggerel to the JCS. Exasperated, Army chief George Marshall despaired, "What is it that causes such complete misunderstandings?" As Buckner's lampoon spread like wildfire through Alaska and the War Department, Marshall and Navy chief Ernest King prepared to discreetly transfer Theobald, Buckner, and Butler out of Alaska in stages. A remorseful Buckner was convinced his Alaskan command was finished, but DeWitt, Theobald, and Buckner eventually cooperated to smooth things over. The sweeping command changes were quietly dropped.

Nevertheless, the USAAF had become disenchanted with the difficult and seemingly deadlocked Alaskan theater. On June 30, the War Department's

The US counteroffensive, June 1942–March 1943

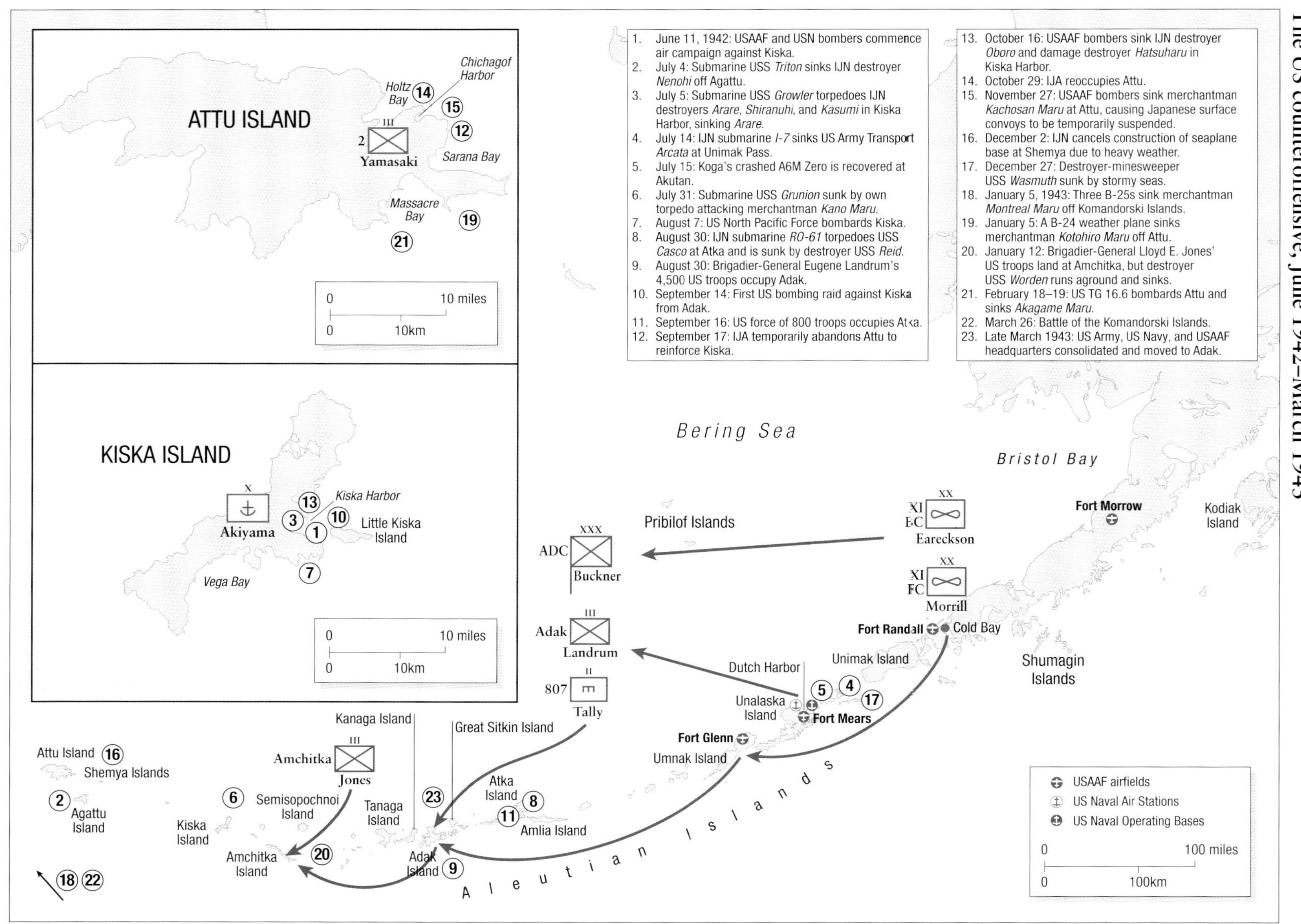

Operations Division had agreed to maintain Alaskan USAAF strength at 24 heavy bombers, 32 medium bombers, 100 fighters, 13 transports, and four observation planes. USAAF chief "Hap" Arnold noted on August 21, "Today we have over 215 aircraft in [Alaska], being contained by less than 50 Japanese aircraft." Emphasizing the theater's poor flying conditions, USAAF brass opposed further air reinforcements as wasteful, claiming Alaska was largely a naval theater where decisive action was unlikely.

A PBY-5A of PatWing-4 loaded with four Mk-37 aerial depth charges. Two more Mk-37s and a 500lb GP bomb are in the foreground. The roundel style and lack of snow suggests the date is autumn 1942. (World War II Database)

On August 29, Commander Tatsudo Tokutomi's *RO-61* snuck into Atka's Nazan Bay where, escorted by destroyer USS *Reid*, seaplane tenders USS *Casco* and USS *Gillis* had recently returned. A vicious storm blew in the following morning and *Reid* departed, opening a favorable tactical situation. After 32 miserable hours on the harbor floor, *RO-61* promptly torpedoed *Casco*, resulting in five killed and 20 wounded; *Casco* ran aground to avoid sinking. Shortly afterwards, depth charges from a PBY and the now-returned *Reid* forced *RO-61* to surface, where she was sunk by gunfire. "Got sub that got you," *Reid* signaled *Casco*, "have five survivors for proof!"

By September 1942, Buckner's Alaska Defense Command would boast 71,500 personnel. Thus encouraged, on July 23 DeWitt and Nimitz had agreed to a westward advance down the Aleutians toward Kiska and Attu. For the initial landing, DeWitt desired Tanaga Island, 200 miles from Kiska; reconnaissance indicated an airfield could be built quickly. Theobald preferred Adak, 50 miles east, for its superior anchorage; the Army believed rugged Adak required two to three months for airfield construction. After an interservice skirmish that went to the JCS, DeWitt reluctantly conceded to Adak. Meanwhile, nearby Atka would become an emergency fighter landing field.

On the night of August 28, submarines USS *Triton* and USS *Tuna* surfaced off Adak. Led by Colonel Lawrence Castner, 38 Alaska Scout commandos paddled to a Kuluk Bay landfall. The following morning, Castner signaled Buckner that Adak was unoccupied. A ragtag collection of 250 barges, scows, floating canneries, and a four-masted schooner duly sortied from Unalaska, carrying Brigadier-General Eugene Landrum's 4,500 US Army troops. They were escorted by US flush-deck destroyers USS *Humphreys*, *King*, *Lawrence*, and *Sands*, Canadian auxiliary cruisers HMCS *Prince David*, *Prince Henry*, and *Prince Robert*, and Canadian corvettes HMCS *Dawson* and *Vancouver*.

On August 30, Landrum's force landed at Adak. Colonel Benjamin Talley's 807th Engineer Aviation Battalion surveyed Adak and chose the only flat spot, a shallow tidal flat at Kuluk Bay's Sweeper Cove. Continuous dawn-till-dusk patrols of B-26 Marauders, P-38 Lightnings, and P-40 Warhawks covered the engineers while they worked. Employing bulldozers and their usual heavy equipment, the 807th transformed the tidal flat. A dike was built, the lagoon drained and leveled, Sweeper Creek re-routed, and infantry press-ganged to lay down the now-ubiquitous pierced-steel plank Marston matting. Adak's

Destroyer USS *Reid* (DD-369) seen in Dutch Harbor on September 6, 1942. She is carrying five Japanese prisoners from her August 31 sinking of submarine *RO-61* at Atka. Behind *Reid* is four-piper destroyer USS *King* (DD-242). (Naval History and Heritage Command)

new airfield was finished in ten days. Eareckson's B-18 Bolo was the first to land on September 10. The crude airstrip was flood prone but functional. Nearby Atka would be occupied by 800 US Army personnel on September 16.

Eleventh Air Force was now just 250 miles from Kiska Harbor; bombers could now be given fighter escort. Employing new low-level tactics, the first Adak-staged strike of 12 B-24s and 28 P-38 and P-39 fighters hit Kiska in unusually clear weather on September 14. Japanese ships, submarines, and installations in Kiska Harbor – "lit up like a Christmas tree" with flak – were attacked by delayed-action 1,000lb bombs and repeatedly strafed by US fighters, including P-39 Airacobras with their heavy 37mm cannon. The Americans inflicted considerable damage, including two Japanese minesweepers sunk; US losses were two P-38s that collided in mid-air.

Weather prevented a repeat until September 25, when ten B-24s, a B-17, and 17 P-40s of Chennault's 343rd Fighter Group and the RCAF's No. 111 Fighter Squadron struck Kiska again. The Japanese scrambled their last two A6M2-N Rufe fighters. Squadron Leader Kenneth Arthur Boomer (RCAF) shot down an A6M2-N Rufe, becoming World War II's first Allied pilot and only Canadian to claim both German and Japanese kills. Moments later, Chennault flamed Kiska's last remaining Rufe while P-40s strafed RO-type submarines. Three days later, one of Chennault's P-40s would sink *RO-65* with a 250lb bomb before being shot down by Japanese flak.

Japanese aerial reconnaissance discovered the new Adak base on September 30. A mere seven Japanese sorties harassed Adak before ceasing October 5. However, on October 16, six B-26 Marauders damaged IJN destroyer *Hatsuharu* in Kiska Harbor and scored a direct hit on destroyer *Oboro*, which exploded and sank without survivors. One B-26 was shot down. Off the Paramushiro coast ten days later, on October 26, submarine USS *S-31* torpedoed and sank 2,864-ton merchantman *Keizan Maru*, inbound to Kiska with supplies. Air operations were temporarily grounded the first week of November, when a severe Aleutian storm whipped up 90mph winds and a foot of water on the Adak airstrip. Attacks resumed on November 9 when four P-38 Lightnings hit Attu, destroying eight A6M2-N Rufes in Holtz Bay.

The Japanese had not been strategically complacent. By fall 1942, IGHQ had scrapped its post-Midway plans to evacuate Kiska and Attu before winter and decided to reinforce the outposts instead. Major-General Kiichiro Higuchi had been named IJA Northern District Army commander in August; unknown to US intelligence, by September 17 Higuchi had temporarily abandoned Attu, transferring its garrison in stages to reinforce Kiska. However, an October 5 survey of nearby Amchitka convinced the Japanese that it was impossible to build an airstrip there. Staging from Paramushiro, Lieutenant-Colonel Isamu Yonegawa's 83rd Independent Infantry Battalion re-occupied Attu on October 29; reinforcements followed over the next several weeks.

On November 1, IGHQ published a joint plan to strengthen Kiska's and Attu's defenses by February 1943, as well as establish a seaplane base at currently unoccupied Shemya. The first Shemya convoy of 1,100 troops departed Paramushiro on November 23. Adak-based USAAF aircraft then sank *Cherrybourne Maru* at Attu on November 27, prompting IGHQ to suspend further surface convoys until the Shemya airbase was established. However, heavy winter weather caused Hosogaya to cancel the Shemya mission on December 2.

USAAF Aleutian Tiger P-40s in a revetment at Adak. Closer to the runway is a B-24 Liberator. Elsewhere the P-40 was well out-classed by this time, but the Warhawk remained happily superior to the only Japanese fighter in theater, the float-equipped A6M-2N Rufe. (PhotoQuest/Getty Images)

After a tactless, inexplicable incident with Colonel Talley that embarrassed the Navy, Nimitz finally relieved Theobald on December 8, although Theobald would retain command until his replacement arrived. The following day, Rear Admiral Charles "Soc" McMorris replaced Rear Admiral "Poco" Smith as North Pacific Force commander. Transfers had reduced McMorris' new command to light cruisers *Detroit* and *Raleigh* and destroyers *Bailey*, *Bancroft*, *Caldwell*, and *Coghlan*. Additionally, off Unimak on December 27, destroyer-minesweeper USS *Wasmuth* was sunk by two exploding depth charges wrenched overboard by stormy seas. No crew were lost.

Despite its reputation as a backwater, between September and December 1942 Alaska had received 16,000 additional troops and 547,000 tons of supplies, compared to the South Pacific Area's 36,000 net personnel and 310,000 tons of cargo. By further comparison, MacArthur's South-West Pacific Area had received only 8,300 men and 157,000 tons of provisions. Additionally, the Army's Seattle Corps of Engineers district had delivered 585,443 tons of construction equipment and materiel to the Alaska Defense Command in 1942, more than triple that of 1941. By January 1, 1943, Buckner would wield 87,000 troops in theater.

Rear Admiral Thomas C. Kinkaid arrived in Kodiak and formally relieved Theobald as North Pacific Area commander on January 4, 1943; TF-8 was accordingly redesignated TF-16. Aggressive, simple, and direct, Kinkaid was a proven fighter and immediately won Buckner's approval. Kinkaid and Buckner began improving Alaska's poor command situation, ordering the separate Navy, Army, and USAAF headquarters consolidated and transferred 1,000 miles forward to Adak, a move to be completed in late March. With the Aleutian campaign escalating, Buckner was promoted lieutenant-general, Butler major-general, and Gehres commodore. Kinkaid promptly submitted a plan to Nimitz and DeWitt for the invasion of Kiska.

The slow strangling of Japanese reinforcements continued. Between December 17 and January 30, 1943, only eight resupply ships would reach

A 54th Fighter Squadron P-38 Lightning receiving maintenance at Adak, late 1942. More famous for other theaters, the P-38's very first aerial victory was scored over the Aleutians on August 4, 1942, when lieutenants Kenneth Ambrose and Stanley Long shot down an H6K Mavis. (PhotoQuest/Getty Images)

Kiska; four reached Attu. Threatened by airstrikes, several marus withdrew only half-unloaded. In January, the Kiska garrison was put under rationing; Attu had been since November. On January 5, three B-25s sank the 6,577-ton *Montreal Maru* off the Komandorski Islands, en route to Kiska with highly trained engineers and their crucial heavy airfield construction equipment. Off Attu two hours later, a B-24 weather plane defied a blizzard to sink the 6,100-ton *Kotohiro Maru*, inbound with provisions. The subsequent dispatch was greeted with an immediate reply from Buckner, who winkingly dubbed it "the best weather report so far rendered in Alaska."

On January 12, 1943, Brigadier-General Lloyd E. Jones' US Army force of 2,100 troops landed at unoccupied Amchitka, supported by McMorris' *Indianapolis*, *Raleigh*, *Detroit*, and four destroyers. However, after landing scouts inside Amchitka's Constantine Harbor, destroyer USS *Worden* was slammed by a sudden current onto a submerged pinnacle, wrecking the ship and killing 14 Americans in 36-degree F water.

The unexpected US occupation of Amchitka, just 50 miles from Kiska, shocked IGHQ. Once an airfield was established, US air attacks would be relentless. The Japanese high command suddenly recognized the North Pacific situation was dire and the Kuriles were now vulnerable. On February 4, 1943, IGHQ ordered Hosogaya and Higuchi "to hold the western Aleutians at all costs and to carry out preparations for war" in the Kuriles. Higuchi planned to reinforce Attu and Kiska to 7,800 troops and have airfields operational on both islands by the end of March.

The Japanese bombed Amchitka with two floatplanes on January 23. Intermittent raids of up to six aircraft eventually damaged construction and killed three US engineers. By January 28, the US airstrip was operational; the following day, a pair of 18th Fighter Squadron P-40Ks downed both A6M2-N Rufes snooping over Amchitka. Japanese raids ended a few weeks later.

Stalking Japanese transports, McMorris' TG-16.6 arrived off Attu the afternoon of February 18 and leisurely shelled Chichagof Harbor and Holtz Bay. *Indianapolis* floatplanes also raided Japanese facilities, but otherwise

The bustling joint US base at Adak, seen in summer 1943. Intended for a *Life* magazine feature, for security reasons this photo was unidentified. Adak became the largest forward US base during the 1942–43 Aleutian campaign; the island's large, fine harbor is visible in the background. (Dmitri Kessel/ The LIFE Picture Collection/ Getty Images)

little damage was observed and the only Japanese resistance was mild anti-aircraft fire. Twenty-three Japanese personnel were killed. Late that night *Indianapolis* and destroyers *Coghlan* and *Gillespie* intercepted the 3,100-ton *Akagame Maru*, en route to Attu with airfield construction equipment and crew. After repeated shell hits and six malfunctioning Mark 15 torpedoes, *Coghlan* and *Gillespie* finally sank *Akagame Maru* with gunfire at 0124hrs, February 19. Two unobserved Japanese transports fled home.

From Amchitka, US fighters and medium bombers were now hitting nearby Kiska up to seven or eight times a day; by late March, the B-17s and B-24s had arrived to add their weight to Kiska's punishment. With only hand tools available, Japanese troops scrambled to build airfields, but "unexpected rocks and poor construction materials" and "increasingly fierce" US air attacks meant Kiska's airstrip would only be half-completed by April 1. Construction proceeded better at Attu, but still not well enough to make the airstrip operational by spring.

Outbound after inserting a reconnaissance team, destroyer USS *Worden* (DD-352) struck a submerged underwater pinnacle off Amchitka the morning of January 12, 1943. She immediately began to sink, suffering 14 dead due to the freezing waters. Though at high cost, *Worden*'s mission however was a success. (Naval History and Heritage Command)

"MY SPEED ZERO": THE BATTLE OF THE KOMANDORSKI ISLANDS, MARCH 26, 1943

Hosogaya decreed surface convoys had become too risky and ordered all resupply attempts be made by inefficient submarines, perturbing the IJA. On March 3, IGHQ forced Hosogaya to dispatch an escorted surface convoy, which successfully reached Attu on March 9. Thus encouraged, IGHQ ordered Hosogaya to make a second surface run to Attu. Hosogaya would depart Paramushiro on March 22 with two heavy cruisers, two light cruisers, and five destroyers – Fifth Fleet's entire strength – escorting two auxiliary cruisers and one transport carrying supplies and 550 troops.

US intelligence had predicted a second IJN convoy run to Attu but had dangerously missed the recent transfers of heavy cruiser *Maya* and light cruiser *Tama* back to Fifth Fleet. Rear Admiral Charles "Soc" McMorris' TG-16.6 was tasked to intercept with heavy cruiser *Salt Lake City*, light cruiser *Richmond*, and destroyers *Bailey*, *Coghlan*, *Dale*, and *Monaghan*. Early on March 26, they found themselves deep in Japanese waters 100 miles southeast of the Soviet Komandorski Islands.

What would follow was a marathon long-range gunnery duel on the deep sea with no submarines or combat aircraft involved – a five-hour anachronism more appropriate for the 19th century than the 20th. The unlikely result would prove strategically decisive for the campaign.

Komandorski Islands order of battle

IJN Fifth Fleet – Vice Admiral Boshiro Hosogaya
- Cruiser Division 21
  - CA *Nachi* (flagship)
  - CA *Maya*
  - CL *Tama*
- Destroyer Division 21
  - DD *Hatsushimo*
  - DD *Wakaba*
- D Convoy – Rear Admiral Tomoichi Mori
  - CL *Abukuma* (flagship)
  - Destroyer Division 6
    - DD *Inazuma*
    - DD *Ikazuchi*
  - AP *Asaka Maru*
  - AP *Sakito Maru*
  - Second Escort Force
    - DD *Usugumo*
  - AP *Sanko Maru*

USN Task Group 16.6 – Rear Admiral Charles H. "Soc" McMorris
- Cruiser Division 1 – McMorris
  - CA *Salt Lake City*
  - CL *Richmond* (flagship)
- Destroyer Squadron 14 – Captain Ralph Riggs
  - DD *Bailey* (flagship)
  - DD *Coghlan*
  - DD *Dale*
  - DD *Monaghan*

After an unscheduled delay, Hosogaya had sent the slower *Sanko Maru* and escorting destroyer *Usugumo* ahead. Hosogaya, riding heavy cruiser *Nachi*, then departed Paramushiro on March 23 with four cruisers, four destroyers, and auxiliary cruisers *Asaka Maru* and *Sakito Maru* to rendezvous with *Sanko Maru* and *Usugumo* 160 miles west of Attu.

At 0730hrs, March 26, McMorris' flagship *Richmond* and destroyer *Coghlan* detected five radar contacts 7–12 miles north. The temperature was 35 degrees F, the seas glassy with a moderate swell. Visibility was clear, with a solid gray overcast at 2,500ft. Dawn was breaking. Admittedly expecting "a Roman holiday," McMorris ordered TG-16.6 to form up around *Richmond* and pursue. Almost simultaneously, Hosogaya's lookouts spotted masts emerging on the horizon. Within minutes, Hosogaya accurately identified McMorris' weaker US force and ordered his four cruisers and four destroyers to turn southeast and engage. Auxiliary cruisers *Asaka Maru* and *Sakito Maru* continued on their original northerly course toward *Sanko Maru* and *Usugumo*.

A B-24 Liberator of the 21st Heavy Bombardment Squadron seen at Amchitka, March 1943. Bombs can be seen loaded on sleds to transport over the snow. At just 50 miles away, Amchitka was actually visible from Kiska's higher elevations on clear days. (Wikimedia Commons/United States Army Air Forces/Public Domain)

Only at 0830hrs did McMorris finally identify two heavy cruisers and two light cruisers during Hosogaya's turn toward TG-16.6. Suddenly, the Americans found themselves badly outmatched far from home. What had been assumed a relatively easy commerce raid had unexpectedly become something much direr. McMorris coolly observed, "The situation had now clarified ... but it had also radically and unpleasantly changed." Overly belligerent after months of tedious patrols, McMorris chose to pursue his

A US 37mm anti-aircraft gun is seen retaliating at a desultory Japanese air raid on Amchitka, early 1943. The Japanese floatplane's bombs can be seen exploding in the harbor. Once an airstrip was successfully built on Amchitka, US air superiority in the Aleutians became overwhelming. (Courtesy of Navy Art Collection, Naval History and Heritage Command)

Battle of the Komandorski Islands, May 26, 1943

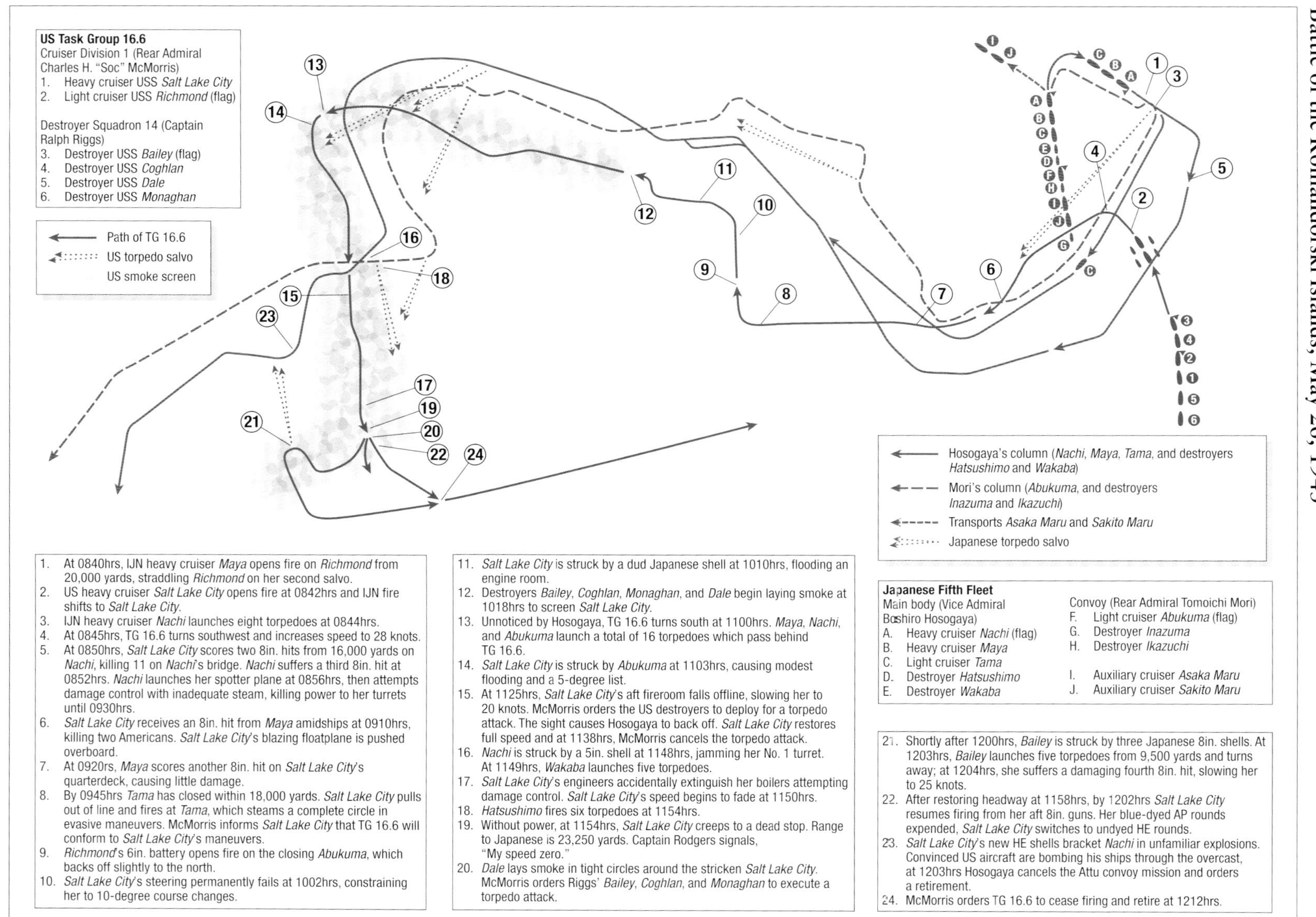

original targets, Hosogaya's fleeing transports. At best TG-16.6 could expect to endure long-range fire from Hosogaya during the stern chase. McMorris duly requested air support from Amchitka and Adak. History's last daylight fleet action was underway.

The two battle fleets converged almost head-on from 40,000 yards and the range closed rapidly. At 0840hrs, *Maya* opened fire on *Richmond* from 20,000 yards, straddling her on the second salvo; in the process *Maya* set her own floatplane afire, which she jettisoned. The Japanese then shifted their fire to the closing *Salt Lake City*, having identified her as a heavy cruiser with longer-ranged 8in. guns. *Salt Lake City* and *Richmond* commenced firing at 0842hrs, followed by the US destroyers' 5in. guns moments later.

Hosogaya's most powerful surface unit at the Komandorski Islands was the Takao-class heavy cruiser *Maya*. Boasting ten 8in. guns and a battery of 24 Type 93 Long Lance torpedoes, the Takaos were among the most fearsome heavy cruisers of World War II. The lead ship is seen underway here in 1932. (World War II Database)

Nachi launched eight Type 93 Long Lance torpedoes at 0844hrs; one would pass beneath *Richmond*'s bow and another broach near *Bailey*. At 0845hrs, McMorris decided, "It seemed expedient to retire," ordering TG-16.6 southwest and increasing speed to 28 knots. Hosogaya matched McMorris' course change. Hosogaya's separate light column, *Abukuma*, and destroyers *Inazuma* and *Ikazuchi*, positioned themselves on McMorris' after starboard quarter, between TG-16.6 and the transports, while Hosogaya deployed his main column of *Nachi*, *Maya*, *Tama*, and destroyers *Hatsushimo* and *Wakaba* on McMorris' after port quarter, between TG-16.6 and Alaska. The Americans' escape route cut off, Hosogaya's superior force began pursuing McMorris' outnumbered flotilla. At 35.5 knots, Hosogaya held a 2–3 knot advantage over TG-16.6, but this was canceled out by the zigzagging required to bring full broadsides to bear during the stern chase. Conversely, the fleeing Americans' masked forward batteries would largely be rendered silent throughout the battle.

Aboard destroyer USS Monaghan, Joseph Candelaria recalled the officers' two black mess attendants "being dragged down to the ammunition lockers. They didn't want to go, they were crying, and I don't blame them, three decks down ... If a shell hit, it would be the end." En route to his fantail battle station, Candelaria ran into a distraught friend: "Kresky told me, 'Look out at them out there, take a look at them,' and he was crying."

At 0850hrs, *Salt Lake City* scored two hits on *Nachi* from 16,000 yards; one 8in. shell smashed *Nachi*'s compass bridge, killing 11, including three men mere yards from Hosogaya, who remained unhurt. The second 8in. shell damaged the base of *Nachi*'s mainmast. *Salt Lake City* scored a third 8in. hit two minutes later, striking *Nachi*'s amidships starboard aircraft deck, killing two and wounding five. At 0856hrs, *Nachi* launched an E13A Jake floatplane from her undamaged port catapult. The Jake would prove the battle's only participating aircraft; its spotting was rendered inconsequential by heavy US anti-aircraft fire. Meanwhile, *Nachi* attempted damage control with inadequate steam, inadvertently killing electrical power to *Nachi*'s turrets and rendering her combat ineffective for half an hour.

Rear Admiral Charles Horatio "Soc" McMorris depicted on the bridge of *Richmond* during the Komandorski Islands battle. Well known for his conspicuous intellect and penetrating questions (hence "Socrates"), McMorris was held in high regard by Nimitz, who tapped McMorris for his personal chief of staff after the Aleutian campaign. (Albert K. Murray Navy Combat Art Center, Washington Navy Yard; NARA)

During the running battle, Salt Lake City's Captain Bertram Rodgers would chase Hosogaya's salvoes with boyish exuberance. "He'd swing right or left," executive officer Worthington S. Bitler recalled, "and the spot we would have been in had we gone the other way would be plowed up with ten or fifteen eight-inch shells." After each miss, Rodgers would flash his Executive Officer a wicked grin: "Fooled them again, Worthy." Bitler agreed. "It was uncanny."

Maya and *Salt Lake City* traded fire until *Maya* scored an 8in. hit on *Salt Lake City*'s amidships catapult at 0910hrs, killing two. The blazing floatplane was pushed overboard. Ten minutes later, *Maya* scored a second, inconsequential 8in. hit on *Salt Lake City*'s quarterdeck.

Running for their lives, at 0920hrs McMorris' TG-16.6 began turning first west, then west-northwest – fleeing, some Americans wondered, toward possible Soviet internment. At 0930hrs, *Nachi* resumed firing. Fifteen minutes later, light cruiser *Tama* had closed within 18,000 yards of *Salt Lake City*. Captain Rodgers wheeled *Salt Lake City* hard over, unmasking his forward guns, and unleashed several 8in. broadsides at *Tama*, which took wild evasive action. McMorris subsequently informed Captain Rodgers that TG-16.6 would conform to *Salt Lake City*'s movements. Meanwhile, light cruiser *Abukuma* and her two destroyers *Inazuma* and *Ikazuchi*, still out of range, continued closing half-heartedly from the Americans' starboard quarter; they would put in a disappointing performance throughout the battle. At 0952hrs, *Salt Lake City*'s gunfire concussions temporarily damaged her own steering control. A minute later, *Richmond*, employing orange-dyed 6in. shells, opened fire on the closing *Abukuma*, which backed off slightly to the north.

By now, *Maya* and *Nachi* had firmly cut off TG-16.6 from Hosogaya's fast-receding transports or any clear escape, positioning themselves 22,000 yards east of *Salt Lake City*. At 1000hrs, a message from Kinkaid announced USAAF bombers were probably four hours away and advised, "Suggest for your consideration retiring action," which reportedly brought laughs on *Richmond*'s bridge.

At 1002hrs, *Salt Lake City*'s problematic steering control failed for good. Now constrained to 10-degree course changes, *Salt Lake City* made an easy target; in the next few minutes, she was bracketed by over 200 Japanese shells. McMorris now decided to disengage however possible, but at 1010hrs, *Salt Lake City* was finally struck from 22,000 yards. The dud shell exited below *Salt Lake City*'s waterline, flooding an engine room. Consequently, at 1018hrs, McMorris' destroyers, remaining between *Salt Lake City* and Hosogaya's fleet, duly laid smoke in the still, humid North Pacific air. *Richmond* trailed 3,000 yards behind.

Through his superior positioning, Hosogaya had forced the Americans, already deep in Japanese waters, to flee west, directly away from Alaska and even deeper toward Kuriles airbases. Yet rather than exploit his superior speed and power to close and annihilate McMorris' TG-16.6, Hosogaya continued zigzagging to bring full broadsides to bear – negating any chance to quickly destroy the Americans, who after an additional turn were now desperately running north-northwest at 30 knots.

The four US destroyers fired furiously. *Monaghan*'s Candelaria recalled, "Gun 4 ... [was] so hot from firing the gun would not fire. So Stofford, [the] Gunners Mate First, he had to hit the damn thing with a sledgehammer in order to make it fire." The mood aboard *Monaghan* was foreboding: "We were scared; a destroyer is only a quarter-inch plate." Water Tender Russell Friesen recalled, "I remember ... I thought I wasn't going to be alive any longer. Or anybody else on that ship."

Cruiser *Salt Lake City* surrounded by TG-16.6's destroyer smoke screen during the March 26, 1943 Komandorski Islands battle. As TG-16.6's only 8in.-gunned cruiser, only *Salt Lake City* possessed the range to threaten Hosogaya's fleet through most of the battle. (Naval History and Heritage Command)

At 1103hrs, *Salt Lake City* suffered a critical 8in. hit, causing 700–1,000 tons flooding and a five-degree list but no loss in speed. Covered by the destroyer smokescreen, TG-16.6 turned south at 1108hrs. Moments later, Hosogaya launched torpedo spreads from *Maya*, *Nachi*, and *Abukuma*; the 16 Long Lances passed harmlessly behind TG-16.6. Crucially, Hosogaya did not immediately register McMorris' southerly turn. As Hosogaya continued on the running battle's earlier westerly course, McMorris' TG-16.6 began to slip away to the south. At 1125hrs, *Salt Lake City*'s flooded after fireroom fell offline and she slowed to 20 knots. McMorris ordered his destroyers to screen *Salt Lake City* with a torpedo attack. The sight of McMorris' destroyers redeploying inspired Hosogaya to execute evasive maneuvers. *Salt Lake City* shortly restored full speed and at 1138hrs, McMorris canceled the torpedo attack.

Events began happening rapidly at 1148hrs, when *Nachi* was hit by a 5in. shell, jamming her No. 1 turret. Destroyer *Wakaba* fired five Long Lances at the US destroyers a minute later, followed at 1154hrs by six from *Hatsushimo*. All missed. Attempting to correct *Salt Lake City*'s five-degree list, at 1150hrs, counterflooding engineers had accidentally let water into the fuel oil lines, extinguishing *Salt Lake City*'s boilers. The cruiser coasted silently on fading momentum, shaken by several Japanese near misses. The next few minutes *Salt Lake City* signaled, "My speed 22 ... My speed 14 ... My speed eight ... My speed four ..." At 1154hrs, *Salt Lake City* crept to a dead stop 23,250 yards from Hosogaya, rocked only by near misses and North Pacific swells. Captain Rodgers hoisted, "My speed zero." A Japanese shell promptly shredded the "zero" flag. Captain Rodgers allegedly ordered, "Abandon ship," but, perhaps mulling the 31-degree F water, seconds later announced "Belay that last word" before it was passed over the intercom.

Destroyer commander Captain Ralph Riggs immediately requested McMorris order a presumably suicidal torpedo attack. McMorris "appeared to mull it over for a moment before he tersely replied, 'Execute.'" Destroyers *Bailey*, *Coghlan*, and *Monaghan* deployed to attack while *Dale* steamed tight circles around the stricken *Salt Lake City*, concealing her with smoke. Riggs signaled: "Targets are the heavies." Watching the destroyers recede toward the horizon, a *Richmond* crewman recalled, "There wasn't a dry eye on

CLIMAX OFF THE KOMANDORSKI ISLANDS, 1203HRS, MARCH 26, 1943 (PP. 60–61)

Heavy cruiser *Nachi* (**1**), Hosogaya's flagship, is seen turning hard to starboard, away from the Americans, as Hosogaya suddenly orders the Attu convoy run aborted. *Nachi* is bracketed by *Salt Lake City*'s unexpected (and undyed) high-explosive rounds (**2**), which appear to be dropped from high overhead by unseen US bombers. The effect is convincing enough that *Nachi*'s anti-aircraft guns begin firing through the low overcast, a spectacle recorded by the Americans.

On the horizon 4.7 miles away, McMorris' destroyers lay smoke as they make their torpedo run toward Hosogaya's cruisers (**3**). Riggs already had *Bailey*'s flag signal to attack ready to hoist before radioing McMorris for permission; some American participants believed it was already flying before McMorris responded. Because Riggs' *Bailey* was in the lead, she outran the three destroyers' combined smokescreen and attracted the bulk of Hosogaya's not-quite-perfect fire. A US destroyerman recalled, "Niagara Falls just off our fantail the entire torpedo run … the Japanese fire solution just never caught up."

Aboard *Nachi*, Japanese officers observed "the valiant United States destroyer" (*Bailey*) disappear time and again in cascades of 8in. shellfire, seemingly for good, only to shockingly reappear as the shell plumes collapsed. After *Bailey* suffered multiple 8in. hits at 1200hrs, Riggs feared *Bailey* might be disabled with her Mk 15 torpedoes still in their tubes and ordered them launched beyond prime range at 1203hrs. None connected. *Bailey*'s last 8in. hit at 1204hrs proved the most damaging, despite being a dud – the flat trajectory of the damage betrayed the Japanese cruiser's point-blank range. A bluejacket kicked the 8in. shell overboard.

Hosogaya had a lot to think about. The Americans had observed *Salt Lake City*'s early 8in. hit on *Nachi*'s bridge at 0850hrs; many felt this hit had noticeably cooled the Japanese commander's aggressiveness for the rest of the battle. After nearly five hours, Hosogaya's cruisers were low on ammunition and his destroyers low on fuel. US bombers were expected overhead at any time, yet Hosogaya was seemingly unable to close or badly damage the Americans. Suddenly dealing with a nerve-racking torpedo attack and apparent US bombing raid simultaneously broke Hosogaya's resolve, saving McMorris' Task Group 16.6 from likely destruction.

"My speed zero." Taken from light cruiser *Richmond*, a stricken and seemingly doomed *Salt Lake City* coasts to a stop shortly after 1154hrs, March 26, 1943 during the climax of the Battle of the Komandorski Islands. The destroyers' smoke screen looms above; beneath *Salt Lake City* lies an unusually calm North Pacific. (Naval History and Heritage Command)

the bridge." McMorris radioed Kinkaid, "*Salt Lake City* stopped. Repeat stopped. *Dale* standing by. Our destroyers attacking."

Aboard *Monaghan*, a chief petty officer recalled, "We had all said good-bye to each other." Down in the engine room, "It was quite an experience," remembered Machinist's Mate Ernest Stahlberg. "The chief engineer came around and shook hands with everybody when we started making our torpedo run." Driving northwest at 37 knots, destroyers *Bailey*, *Coghlan*, and *Monaghan* made flank speed toward Hosogaya's battle line, Riggs' *Bailey* in the lead. During their charge, *Bailey* and *Monaghan* concentrated their 5in. fire on heavy cruiser *Nachi* while *Coghlan* dueled heavy cruiser *Maya*. Aboard *Nachi*, Commander Kintaro Miura praised the US destroyers' gunnery, claiming 5in. shells "landed aboard like rain."

Hosogaya shifted fire to the imminent threat of the US destroyers. Aboard *Monaghan*'s bridge, Signalman Frank Andrews counted over 125 shell splashes sprouting about *Bailey* and *Coghlan*. Just after 1200hrs, at a range of 10,000 yards, *Bailey* was hammered by three 8in. shells from *Nachi* and *Maya*. *Nachi*'s Miura marveled he "did not know how a ship could live through the concentration of fire brought to bear on the leading destroyer."

Staggering beneath the onslaught, *Bailey* launched five torpedoes from 9,500 yards (4.7 miles) and turned away at 1203hrs. Seconds later, *Bailey* received a fourth 8in. hit, slowing her to 25 knots and knocking out her gyro, radars, an engine, and power to guns and director. Japanese lookouts spotted four torpedo wakes but none connected.

Aboard *Nachi*, however, Hosogaya was nervous. He had intercepted McMorris' call for air support three and a half hours earlier; by Hosogaya's reckoning, USAAF bombers should be arriving any minute, completely unseen above the low overcast. Meanwhile, from 13 miles away, it was simply not apparent the hull-down, smoke-concealed *Salt Lake City* was dead in the water. Incredibly, Hosogaya's spotter plane registered *Salt Lake City*'s plight but made no report until landing at Attu hours later.

Yet deep within *Salt Lake City*, Captain Rodgers' prize-winning engineering crew had restored power. By 1158hrs, *Salt Lake City* was once again making headway. At 1202hrs, Captain Rodgers resumed firing from his after 8in. guns, their 256lb shells having long been transferred aft by

Dusted by snow flurries, cruiser USS *Salt Lake City*'s 8in./55-caliber gun barrels display heat-scaled paint from extensive firing during the March 26 battle. Below the guns, open-bottomed life rafts betray the futility of abandoning ship on the North Pacific. This photo, taken several days after the battle and frequently unidentified, is a favorite of many warship books. (Naval History and Heritage Command)

hand from turret No. 2. *Salt Lake City* had expended her blue-dyed armor-piercing rounds; her 8in. magazines were now down to their final 15 percent – undyed high-explosive shells. One minute later, *Nachi* was suddenly bracketed by huge, brilliant white geysers of a new type. *Nachi*'s anti-aircraft guns erupted skyward toward the US aircraft presumably bombing through the overcast. Already low on fuel and ammunition (but not so low as McMorris), Hosogaya's nerve broke. At 1203hrs, Hosogaya ordered the Attu run aborted.

The last Japanese shells landed near *Salt Lake City* at 1204hrs. Three minutes later, *Salt Lake City* had worked up to 17 knots. On the horizon, stupefied Americans observed what seemed a miracle – the Japanese were withdrawing. Riggs signaled McMorris incredulously: "The enemy is retiring to the west. Shall I follow them?" As range and angle increased, *Coghlan* and *Monaghan* turned back with their torpedoes still in their tubes. By 1212hrs, Hosogaya was out of range. TG-16.6 ceased fire and retired due east at 20 knots. A relieved Kinkaid ordered McMorris back to Adak. Ironically, an embarrassing series of logistical, mechanical, and weather foul-ups meant Butler's bombers were still on the ground.

Nachi, *Salt Lake City*, and *Bailey* had been seriously damaged. Japanese losses were 14 killed, 26 wounded, while American casualties were seven killed and 20 wounded. McMorris (and flagship *Richmond*) received substantial criticism from American participants for questionable actions during the battle, but McMorris' absent superiors Nimitz and Kinkaid praised McMorris for a glorious victory. By contrast, Hosogaya returned to Paramushiro on March 28 and was forced into retirement. Vice Admiral Shiro Kawase assumed Fifth Fleet command on April 1. Attu had last received a surface resupply ship on March 9; McMorris' unlikely victory proved it the last.

OPERATION *LANDCRAB*: THE BATTLE OF ATTU, MAY 11–30, 1943

Major-General Higuchi had appointed Colonel Yasuyo Yamasaki commander 2nd District, North Seas Garrison (Hokkai Shubitai) in February 1943. Yamasaki would be inserted into Attu by submarine on April 17 to assume command from Lieutenant-Colonel Isamu Yonegawa. However, the following day Admiral Yamamoto was killed over the South Pacific by US P-38 Lightnings, throwing Japanese plans and leadership into disarray. Meanwhile, Kawase continued Hosogaya's "watchful waiting" strategy, hoping late May's summer fog would conceal Aleutian resupply convoys.

Liberating Kiska required US forces from outside Alaska. After a heated confrontation with the War Department, DeWitt had reluctantly accepted Major-General Albert Brown's 7th Motorized Division, desert-trained in California for North Africa combat. Aware of the Aleutians' uniquely challenging conditions, DeWitt requested he be allowed to replace Brown as 7th Division commander with an Aleutian veteran, Major-General Charles Corlett. When the War Department refused, DeWitt asked to at least replace Brown's deputy with an Aleutian veteran, Brigadier-General Eugene Landrum, but this suggestion was also ignored.

Japan's final Attu commander, Colonel Yasuyo Yamasaki, seen in a posthumously doctored photo. Yamasaki had in fact been aboard the March 26, 1943 Attu convoy which was turned back at the Battle of the Komandorski Islands. Yamasaki came late to the Aleutian campaign, but he would sell Attu dearly. (Wikimedia Commons/Public Domain)

On January 15, Brown's vehicle-stripped 7th Division began amphibious training at Fort Ord, California under USMC Major-General Holland M. "Howlin' Mad" Smith's improvised staff of amphibious, naval, and Alaskan experts. Lacking invasion shipping, in early March, Kinkaid recommended instead invading Attu, whose strength was estimated at just 500 personnel. After DeWitt promised Attu would be taken in three days, the JCS authorized the Attu invasion on March 22. By April, Kinkaid's Attu estimates were revised upwards to 1,587 Japanese defenders. Three additional transports became available and the entire redesignated 7th Infantry Division was committed to Operation *Landcrab*, to be transported by Rear Admiral Francis Rockwell's California-based TF-51.

Kinkaid's *Landcrab* naval forces included the Alaska-based TF-16 (North Pacific Force) and Rockwell's TF-51. TF-16 would clinch Attu's blockade via Rear Admiral Robert Giffen's Northern Covering Group (heavy cruisers USS *Wichita*, *Louisville*, and *San Francisco*, four destroyers), and McMorris' Southern Covering Group (light cruisers USS *Detroit*, *Richmond*, and *Santa Fe*, five destroyers). TF-16's landing support groups included destroyer USS *Phelps*, gunboat USS *Charleston*, Canadian corvettes HMCS *Dawson* and *Vancouver*, three submarines, six minecraft, six tankers, four LSTs, eight LCT(5)s, and 11 PT boats. TF-16's Attu Reinforcement Group included five transports and three freighters.

Rockwell's TF-51 comprised aging battleships USS *Pennsylvania*, *Idaho*, and *Nevada*, escort carrier USS *Nassau* (29 F4F Wildcat fighters and one SOC Seagull of VC-21 and VMO-155), ten destroyers, four destroyer-minesweepers, one destroyer minelayer, and – carrying Brown's Landing Force Attu – attack transports USS *Zeilin*, *J. Franklin Bell*, *Harris*, and *Heywood*, chartered civilian freighter SS *Perida*, and destroyer-transport USS *Kane*. On April 24, TF-51's inadequate, overcrowded transports departed San Francisco for Cold Bay, Alaska with Brown's Landing Force Attu aboard. Inexplicably, Brown's men had been issued minimal cold-weather clothing. They would fight in Attu's wet, freezing, windswept conditions not with parkas and rubber shoepac footwear, but standard field jackets and leather blucher boots.

By April, Eleventh Air Force strength averaged 226 aircraft. A 115mph blizzard had enveloped the Aleutians the first week of April, followed by excellent flying weather that allowed 1,175 sorties. However, localized fog reduced Attu sorties to 30. Kiska flak claimed a B-24 and a P-40; another nine fighters were lost to operational causes. By now, the bustling US joint headquarters at Adak hosted 19,067 US Army and 7,811 US Navy

Escort carrier USS *Nassau* (ACV-16) off Attu, May 1943. *Nassau* was the first escort carrier (auxiliary carrier) to be used in a Pacific amphibious support role. Attu's mercurial fog conditions allowed only small, fleeting flight windows, forcing *Nassau* to station just offshore to exploit CAS requests. *Nassau* never flew more than eight Wildcats simultaneously to avoid leaving fighters stranded aloft by unpredictable fog, unable to land. (US Navy and Marine Corps Museum/ Naval Aviation Museum/ NavSource.org)

personnel; at Amchitka were 10,260 US Army troops and 903 US Navy officers and men, as well as a brand new 5,000ft airstrip. Meanwhile, Kinkaid ordered McMorris to bombard Attu a second time. *Landcrab*'s Southern Covering Force opened a 25-minute shelling of Holtz Bay and Chichagof Harbor at 0815hrs, April 26. Damage was moderate, but soon repaired.

After May 1 debarkation drills, poor weather scrubbed TF-51's May 3 sortie, delaying D-Day from May 7 to May 8. TF-51 departed Cold Bay on May 4. Once at sea, storms again postponed D-Day to May 11. On May 7, to intercept a suspected counterattack, Rockwell sent *Pennsylvania*, *Idaho*, and *Nevada*'s TG-51.1 prowling through fierce seas west of Attu with McMorris' Southern Covering Force. Returning empty-handed, TG-51.1 made a fog-choked rendezvous with the invasion fleet 115 miles north of Attu late on May 10. After colliding in the fog, minelayer *Sicard* towed destroyer *MacDonough* back to Adak. Late that evening, TF-51 began its overnight run-in to Attu.

Operation *Landcrab* orders of battle

IJA 2nd District, North Seas Garrison (Hokkai Shubitai) – Colonel Yasuyo Yamasaki
83rd Independent Infantry Battalion – Lieutenant-Colonel Isamu Yonegawa
303rd Independent Infantry Battalion – Major Jokuji Watanabe
Aoto Provisional Anti-Aircraft Battalion
Northern Kurile Fortress Infantry Battalion
6th Independent Mountain Artillery
302nd Independent Engineer Company

US Landing Force Attu (US 7th Infantry Division) – Major-General Albert Brown
Provisional Scout Battalion – Captain William H. Willoughby
- 7th Scout Company
- 7th Cavalry Reconnaissance Troop

Northern Force – Colonel Frank L. Culin
- 1st/17th Regimental Combat Team

Southern Force – Colonel Edward Palmer Earle
- 2nd/17th Regimental Combat Team
- 3rd/17th Regimental Combat Team
- 2nd/32nd Regimental Combat Team

Reinforcements/Combat Support
- 1st/32nd Regimental Combat Team
- 3rd/32nd Regimental Combat Team
- 1st/4th Regimental Combat Team (at Adak)
- 78th Coast Artillery (Anti-Aircraft) Regiment
- 50th Combat Engineer Battalion

Desolate and perpetually fog-shrouded Attu, 35 miles long by 15 miles wide, rises as sheer ocean cliffs to a tangled topographic mess of deep, soggy valleys, clear-flowing creeks, and steep ravines slicing through jagged, snow-covered 3,000ft mountains. Just 5 percent of Attu's ragged coastline is actual beach. Landings demanded approaches over submerged, uncharted reefs. Annual precipitation averages 40–50in., falling as mist or snow five to six days per week. Regional May 1, 1943 snow cover descended to 200ft above sea level. Daily highs during *Landcrab* would average a damp 25–37 degrees F. Lows would fall to 10 degrees F. Lichens, moss, tundra, and the occasional low shrub comprised Attu's natural cover. The island's combined snow cover and thick, taffy-like muskeg could only be traversed on foot, exhaustingly, at about 1.5 mph. The under-clothed Americans could expect to burn over 4,000 calories per day in Attu's winter combat conditions.

Yamasaki's garrison actually totaled 2,614 half-starving troops – mostly infantry but including anti-aircraft batteries (totaling twelve 75mm anti-aircraft guns, six Type 98 20mm machine cannons, and six Type 93 13.2mm machine guns), four 75mm pack howitzers, and IJA and IJN support attachments.

Lieutenant-Colonel Isamu Yonegawa's 83rd Infantry Battalion defended the northern Holtz Bay sector, including Yamasaki's headquarters. Yonegawa's total forces were three companies of infantry, engineers, and naval support personnel, along with two anti-aircraft companies and two 75mm pack howitzers.

Major Jokuji Watanabe's 303rd Infantry Battalion defended the southern Massacre Bay–Chichagof Harbor sector, including the vital Jarmin Pass (Massacre–Holtz Pass) and Clevesy Pass (Massacre–Sarana Pass), both of which bisected eastern Attu. Defending Jarmin Pass was Captain Toshio Hayashi's 1st Company/303rd, including a platoon positioned in Massacre Valley as a delaying force. Lieutenant Honna's 2nd Company/303rd defended Clevesy Pass, supported by Lieutenant Goto's 4th Company/303rd from Gilbert Ridge, which divided Massacre Valley and Sarana Valley.

Throughout Attu, well-sited machine-gun, mortar, and 75mm emplacements lurked unseen above the fog line atop steep ridges, offering enfilading plunging fire of the deep valleys and passes below. IJN plans to operate 48 A6M Zeroes from Attu were ruined by Holtz Bay's still-incomplete airstrip. G4M Betty bombers were in range from Paramushiro, but Kawase's Fifth Fleet had been gutted to a paltry few surface ships and submarines. All supplies had been severed; since April 1, rice rations had been reduced to less than a pint a day. Yamasaki was given the slim hope of an IJN rescue mission in late May.

Conversely, US power was ascendant. Brown's total troop strength off Attu was 11,000; floating reserves at Adak pushed this to 16,000. Landing Force Attu had been well trained in amphibious landings, although Brown's men remained woefully unprepared for Attu's environment. Forward-based USAAF strength on May 11 comprised 80 P-40s, 26 P-38s, three F-5As, 28 B-24s, and 31 B-25s, totaling 168 aircraft (109 fighters and 59 bombers). Commodore Gehres'

Maintaining the Attu blockade, heavy cruisers USS *Louisville* and USS *San Francisco* of Giffen's Northern Covering Group patrol the Bering Sea in May 1943. Sealing an invasion area off from counter-invasions is an important but often overlooked aspect of amphibious operations. (World War II Database)

A US freighter docked at the Adak pier in an oil painting by William Draper. Supplies, munitions, and a floating reserve battalion, Alaska Defense Command's BCT 4-1, were kept ready for *Landcrab* at the main US base at Adak, 430 miles east of Attu. (Courtesy of Navy Art Collection, Naval History and Heritage Command)

PatWing-4 had been expansively reorganized on November 1, 1942 and redesignated Fleet Air Wing Four (FAW-4). Gehres' 24 PV-1 Venturas, 30 PBY Catalinas, and five seaplane tenders would handle patrols and ASW duty.

Attu's precise interior topography was unknown to the Americans. Poor intelligence demanded five separate US invasion plans, all relying on a single US Coast & Geodetic Survey chart. Rockwell and Brown chose Plan E. Northern Force would land with 3,000 troops in the north off Holtz Bay, while Southern Force with the main strength of 8,000 would land at Massacre Bay. The two arms would then converge in Attu's unmapped interior to trap and subsequently drive the Japanese into Chichagof Harbor for the kill. Kinkaid would exercise overall *Landcrab* command from Adak, 430 miles away. Rockwell's flagship *Pennsylvania* would station off northern Attu, while from southern Attu Brown would command US forces ashore. Unfortunately, high-latitude atmospherics would scramble US radio transmissions, while Aleutian fog enveloped visual signals, couriers, and aircraft. Consistently wretched US communications would play a significant factor in the battle's development.

Having dropped anchor miles off Attu, attack transport USS *Heywood* (APA-6) deploys her still largely empty LCVPs on D-Day. They will shortly be loaded by US infantrymen scrambling over rope ladders. Note the thick fog, obscuring visibility even at short ranges. (Naval History and Heritage Command)

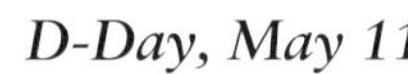

D-Day, May 11

At 0200hrs, May 11, *Nassau* F4F Wildcats bombed and strafed Chichagof Harbor and scattered leaflets demanding surrender. An hour later, inserted by submarines USS *Nautilus* and USS *Narwhal*, 229 members of Captain Willoughby's 7th Scout Company paddled rubber boats through 27-degree F fog to Beach Scarlet, northwest of Holtz Bay. Willoughby's Scouts, extraordinarily heavily armed at the expense of rations, would reconnoiter Beach Scarlet for large-scale landing suitability, then drive south to contain any Japanese attempt to escape west. Aboard destroyer USS *Kane*, Willoughby's 165 Scouts of Captain Austin's 7th

Reconnaissance Troop were delayed landfall by fog. Battleship *Pennsylvania* eventually guided *Kane* to landfall by radar, and shortly before noon, Austin's 7th Reconnaissance Troop would follow Willoughby at Beach Scarlet.

By 0927hrs, destroyer USS *Phelps* had led eight LCVPs of Alaska Scouts to Beach Red to reconnoiter; among their number were Northern Force commander Colonel Frank Culin and beachmaster Commander "Squeaky" Anderson. However, their transmissions never reached Northern Force offshore. At 1350hrs, after multiple queries to Brown off southern Attu went unanswered, transport commander Captain Patrick Buchanan (USN) independently ordered USS *J. Franklin Bell* to begin landing Northern Force. *Phelps*, her signal light only visible within 600 yards, led in the first wave of 29 LCVPs at 1410hrs. At 1615hrs, Lieutenant-Colonel Albert Hartl's BCT 17-1 began landing at Beach Red.

Visibility was too poor to offer direct fire support, so *Pennsylvania* and *Idaho* opened radar-directed fire on Chichagof Harbor batteries at 1510hrs. Meanwhile, US Coast & Geodetic Survey ship USCGS *Hydrographer*, directly exposed to Japanese artillery, began a methodical sounding of Attu's unknown shallows. At 1825hrs *Pennsylvania* evaded a PBY-spotted torpedo. Eleventh Air Force had dropped 95 tons of bombs on Attu since May 1 but none since May 6 because of the murk. On D-Day, frustrated Eleventh Air Force sorties reported 9/10ths cloud cover and ground fog to 1,500ft.

Yamasaki had known TF-51 was at sea. Accordingly, on May 3 Yamasaki had suspended all airfield and fortification construction and deployed

Underdressed US troops from transport USS *Heywood* climb down a cargo net into an LCM during *Landcrab*'s initial D-Day landings, May 11. To the standard amphibious landing hazards *Landcrab* also added wet, freezing cold and fog. (Naval History and Heritage Command)

Destroyer USS *Pruitt* (DD-347) leads transport USS *Heywood*'s LCVPs through nine miles of thick fog to a D-Day landing at Massacre Bay, May 11, 1943. One LCVP would swamp en route to the beach when its bow-ramp dropped inadvertently, drowning four Americans. (Naval History and Heritage Command)

Battleship USS *Pennsylvania* (BB-38) unleashes her main battery of twelve 14in. guns against Japanese positions on northern Attu, May 1943. Rockwell's flagship had been quickly repaired after Pearl Harbor but along with *Nevada* (BB-36) and *Idaho* (BB-42) had spent long months tied up at San Francisco piers, where they were derisively called the "Market Street Commandos." The three battleships finally returned to action for Operation *Landcrab*. (Naval History and Heritage Command)

personnel to forward positions. However, with no invasion by May 9, Yamasaki had been forced to relax his posture and recall his exhausted men. The May 11 US landings therefore achieved tactical surprise. An IJA corporal recalled the strangeness of US ships and aircraft swarming Attu, but not shelling or strafing like usual. A Daihatsu boat was dispatched to investigate: "They returned almost at once in a hurry. Over in the west arm of Holtz Bay the enemy was landing. When we heard this everyone's face went pale – it was not what we were expecting."

At 1500hrs, Yamasaki had ordered defensive positions again reinforced and classified documents burned. Yamasaki held the vital passes and did so at altitudes above the fog line where US field artillery, air support, and naval gunfire could not easily be brought to bear. Shortly after 1800hrs, Yonegawa's 75mm anti-aircraft battery at Holtz Bay opened fire on BCT 17-1's beach patrol. BCT 17-1's main strength had already scaled the 250ft beach escarpment immediately inland and continued to advance undetected toward 800ft Hill X, two miles south of Beach Red.

Willoughby's exhausted Scouts had been climbing all day from Beach Scarlet up a steep valley. At 2,500ft above sea level, the advance 7th Scout Company had reached the assumed summit of the pass; further inland their maps were blank. Willoughby ordered the Scouts halted for the night. By 2100hrs, Northern Force had landed 1,500 men – 400 at Beach Scarlet and 1,100 at Beach Red. By 2230hrs, darkness and fog reduced visibility to zero and BCT 17-1 dug in for the night, unsure of its location.

Meanwhile, Southern Force's 0740hrs H-Hour had been delayed by persistent fog. Finally, Rockwell had ordered landings to commence at 1530hrs regardless. Lieutenant James Mahoney's 4th Platoon of the 7th Reconnaissance Troop landed at southeast Massacre Bay's Alexai Point at 1555hrs. By establishing outposts across the East Cape Peninsula, they would cover Southern Force's rear. Around 1620hrs, Southern Force's BCT 17-3 and 17-2 had begun landing at Massacre Bay's Beach Yellow and Beach Blue. IJA Captain Toshio Hayashi had posted a platoon of his 1st Company/303rd at Massacre Bay to warn of a US landing. Above Massacre Beach, two Japanese 20mm machine cannon were perfectly sited to harass the landings, but their crews fled. BCT 17-3 and BCT 17-2 would advance abreast up Massacre Valley, on the left and right respectively; BCT 17-2 hugged the low Hogback Ridge dividing Massacre Valley. Southern Force's objectives in Attu's interior were Jarmin Pass to the north, and Clevesy Pass to the northeast. Once these passes were taken, Attu would be sliced in half.

At 1730hrs, the 48th Field Artillery Battalion's first 105mm battery landed at Massacre Bay, sticking fast in the beach's soggy quagmire. Thirty minutes later, the immobilized 105mms opened fire on a reported IJA mortar position above and destroyed it. Meanwhile, BCT 17-2 had advanced 2,500 yards up Massacre Valley before being stopped by IJA rifle and machine-gun fire from high up on Gilbert Ridge to their right.

By 2100hrs, Southern Force had landed 2,000 at Massacre Bay, totaling 3,500 US troops ashore. Brown came ashore at 2300hrs and established his command post at Massacre Bay's Beach Yellow. Indirect fire from observer-directed US artillery would eventually prove a significant factor in the battle, while driving US tractors through the island's gravel-bedded creeks proved a partial solution to Attu's immobilizing surface muck.

The battles for Holtz Bay and Jarmin Pass, May 12–18

Submarines *I-31*, *I-34*, and *I-35* had sortied from Kiska to counterattack TF-51. Prowling for *Pennsylvania*'s D-Day assailant, two destroyers and a PBY forced *I-35* to the surface at midnight, May 11/12. *I-35* then submerged beneath *Edwards'* and *Farragut's* gunfire and escaped. Hours later, *I-35* would unsuccessfully fire torpedoes at light cruiser *Santa Fe*, while *Pennsylvania* would again just miss being torpedoed by *I-31*.

As dawn broke on May 12, battleships *Pennsylvania* and *Idaho* bombarded Holtz Bay's anti-aircraft batteries from 14,000 yards, while battleship *Nevada*'s 14in. guns opened fire on the steep ridges above Massacre Valley. A forward observer reported, "Dead Japanese, hunks of artillery, pieces of guns, and arms and legs rolled down out of the fog on the mountain."

In the north, Willoughby's Scouts resumed their march at 0400hrs, May 12. They quickly summited the pass. Making excellent time downhill in the snow, they reached the rear of Japanese positions at 0800hrs and attacked toward Holtz Bay and the Scout Company's scheduled link-up with Hartl's BCT 17-1. Willoughby's Scouts then called in strikes on Japanese anti-aircraft batteries. Twenty-four P-38s dropped 500lb bombs and 23lb parafrags over Chichagof and Holtz Bay from low altitude, then strafed Japanese positions under heavy anti-aircraft fire. The P-38 strikes were followed by 18 B-24s and B-25s. Strong Japanese resistance halted Willoughby's advance for the next three days and Willoughby's Scouts dug in.

The morning of May 12, Hartl's BCT 17-1 had resumed its attack against Hill X, defended by Yonegawa's Kobayashi and Sato detachments. Around 0900hrs, these detachments caught Hartl's attacking Company A in the open. Company A scrambled to the desperate cover of a deep ravine in no man's land, where they were inevitably pinned by severe Japanese heavy weapons fire. Barrages from beach-bound 105mm howitzers, naval fire support from destroyer USS *Phelps*, and *Nassau* Wildcat strafing runs combined to cover BCT 17-1 as Hartl broke through to his trapped Company A at 1700hrs. BCT 17-1 then overwhelmed the initial Japanese defense line and captured Hill X.

A US mortar team offers infantry fire support at Attu, May 1943. Several critical *Landcrab* elements are visible here: Attu's steep, rugged mountains, a dusting of recent snowfall, and the inadequate clothing of US front-line troops fighting through the wet, wintry conditions. A decisive explanation for the comprehensive US winter-equipping failure remains contentious and unresolved. (Imperial War Museum, OEM 6284)

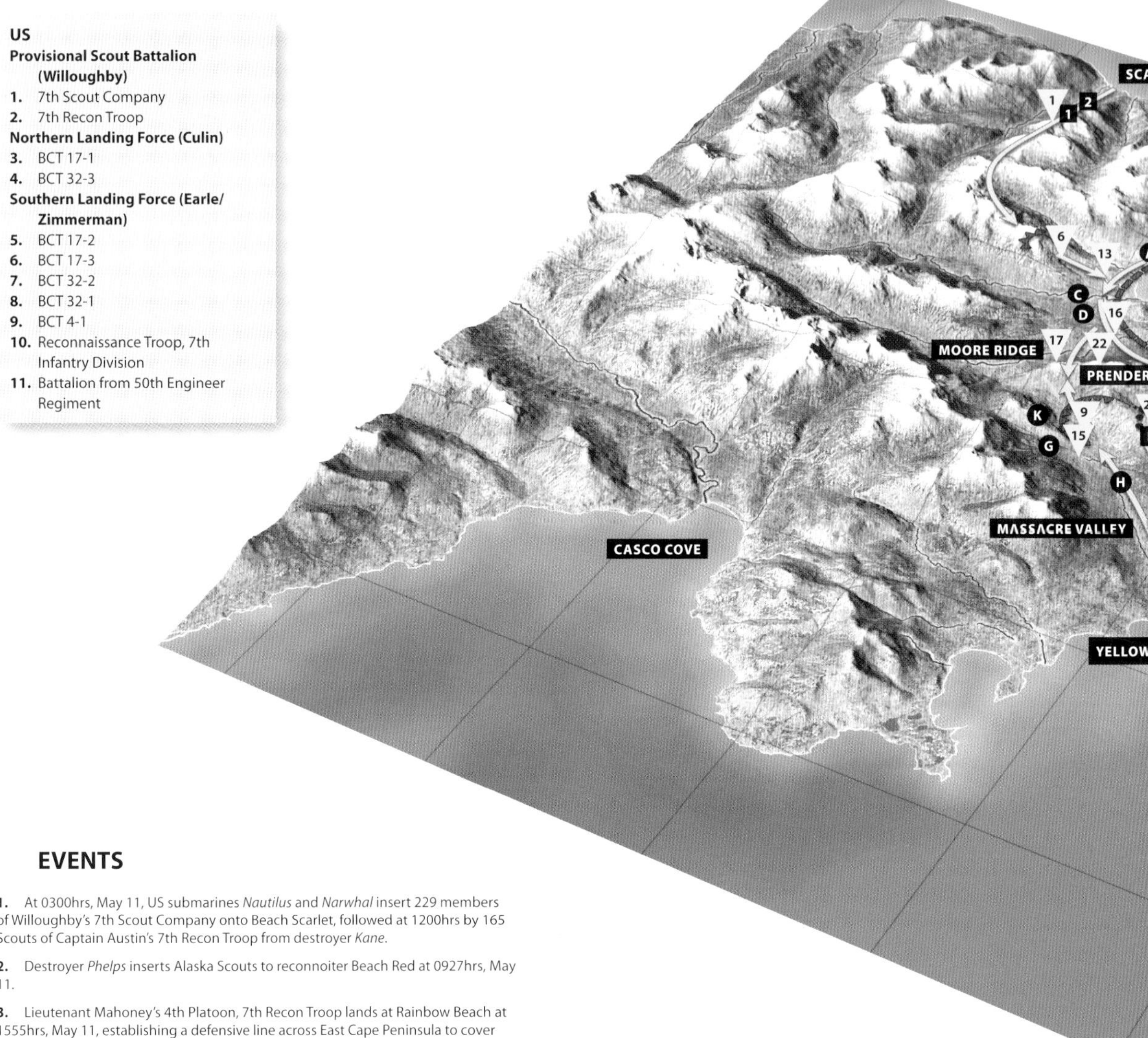

EVENTS

1. At 0300hrs, May 11, US submarines *Nautilus* and *Narwhal* insert 229 members of Willoughby's 7th Scout Company onto Beach Scarlet, followed at 1200hrs by 165 Scouts of Captain Austin's 7th Recon Troop from destroyer *Kane*.

2. Destroyer *Phelps* inserts Alaska Scouts to reconnoiter Beach Red at 0927hrs, May 11.

3. Lieutenant Mahoney's 4th Platoon, 7th Recon Troop lands at Rainbow Beach at 1555hrs, May 11, establishing a defensive line across East Cape Peninsula to cover Southern Force.

4. Lieutenant-Colonel Hartl's BCT 17-1 begins landing at Beach Red at 1615hrs, May 11.

5. Colonel Earle's BCT 17-3 and 17-2 land at beaches Yellow and Blue at 1620hrs to no opposition. BCT 17-2 is eventually stopped 2,500 yards up Massacre Valley by Japanese fire from Gilbert Ridge.

6. Willoughby's Scouts attack Japanese positions on May 12, the beginning of three days of fiercely contested stalemate.

7. The morning of May 12, Hartl's BCT 17-1 attacks Hill X, defended by Lieutenant-Colonel Yonegawa's Kobayashi and Sato detachments, capturing it in heavy fighting that evening.

8. Transport *Perida* lands BCT 32-2 in Massacre Bay at 1140hrs, May 12.

9. Captain Hayashi's 1st Company/303rd halts Earle's Southern Force in Massacre Valley by May 12. Colonel Earle is killed and replaced by Colonel Zimmerman.

10. Transport *U.S. Grant* lands BCT 32-1 at Massacre Bay on May 13.

11. Under heavy fire, transport *Chirikof* lands BCT 32-3 at Beach Red by 1730hrs, May 13.

12. Threatened by Northern Force, Colonel Yamasaki orders Japanese Holtz Bay forces to withdraw toward Fishhook Ridge and Sarana Pass the morning of May 14.

13. No longer facing resistance, Willoughby's Scouts rendezvous with Culin's Northern Force at 1530hrs, May 15.

14. On May 16, Kinkaid relieves Major-General Brown of Attu Force command. His replacement, Brigadier-General Landrum, arrives and takes command at 1700hrs15. Yamasaki withdraws Hayashi's 1st Company/303rd from Jarmin Pass on May 16.

16. Northern Force attacks an evacuated Moore Ridge at 0010hrs, May 17. Within hours all Holtz Bay is in US hands.

17. Southern Force summits the now-evacuated Jarmin Pass and links up with Northern Force in the early morning of May 18.

18. BCT 17-1 assaults Prendergast Ridge on May 19; it will not be cleared until May 25.

19. BCT 17-2 attacks Clevesy Pass at 0952hrs, May 19. BCT 4-1 lands at Massacre Bay on May 20, relieves BCT 17-1 at the front, and clears Clevesy Pass.

20. Late on May 21, BCT 32-2 destroys Lieutenant Honna's heavily entrenched 2nd Company/303rd, winning 2,000ft Point Able.

21. BCT 17-3 attacks Sarana Nose at 0640hrs, May 22, taking it with few casualties.

22. On May 22, BCT 4-1 conquers the crest of Prendergast Ridge.

23. Fifteen G4M bombers unsuccessfully attack gunboat *Charleston* and destroyer *Phelps* in Holtz Bay at 1548hrs, May 22. The following day, five P-38s shoot down 12 of 19 G4M bombers, losing two P-38s.

24. At 1000hrs, May 24, combined US forces begin attacking the Fishhook, conquering it May 28.

25. BCTs 32-1 and 32-2 assault Buffalo Ridge, partially claiming the crest by nightfall, May 28.

26. Yamasaki's last-ditch, 800-strong banzai charge from Chichagof Harbor opens at 0030hrs, May 29. Desperate fighting breaks the banzai charge at Engineer Hill, ending organized Japanese resistance on Attu.

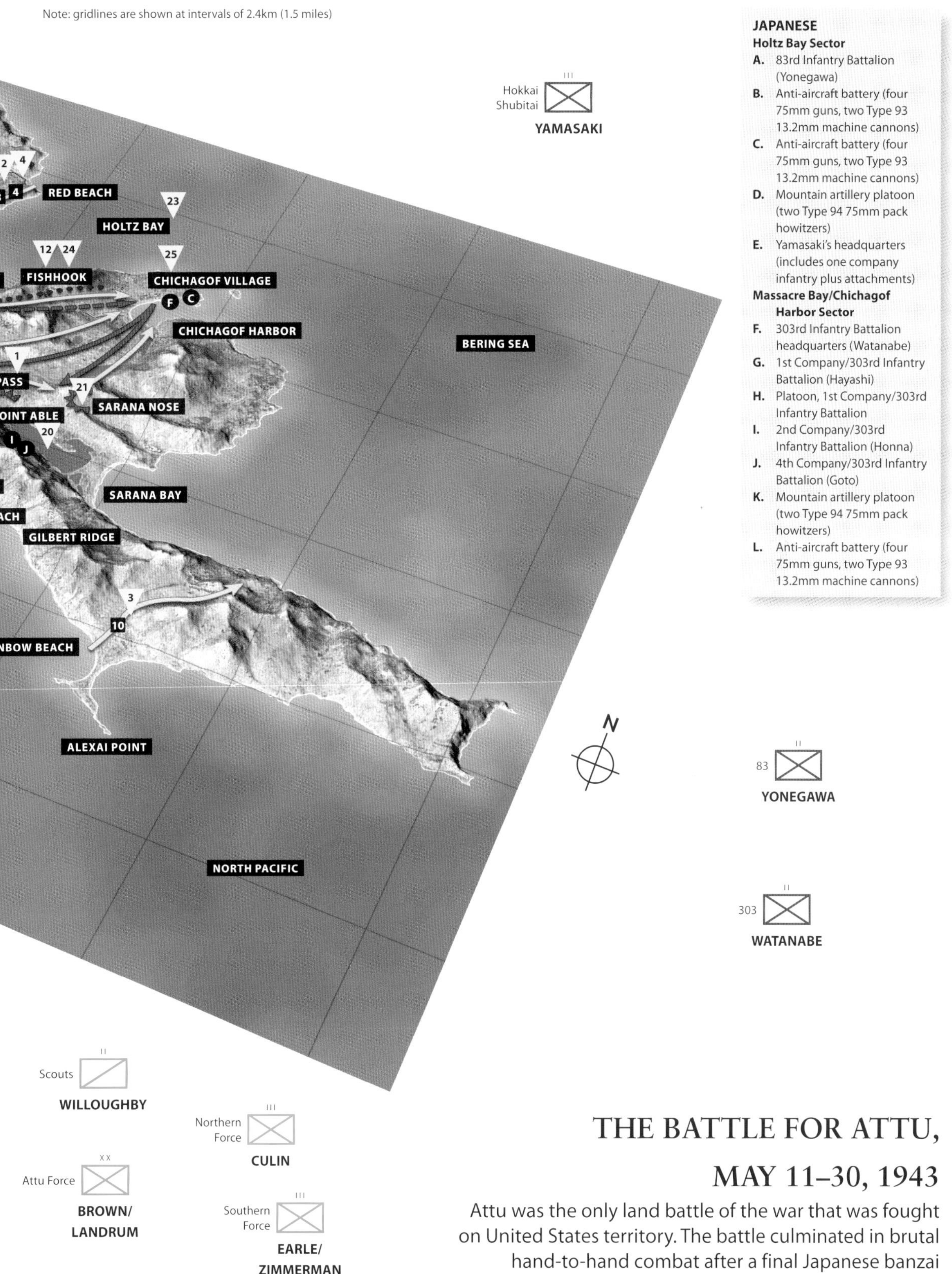

THE BATTLE FOR ATTU, MAY 11–30, 1943

Attu was the only land battle of the war that was fought on United States territory. The battle culminated in brutal hand-to-hand combat after a final Japanese banzai charge broke through American lines.

US troops unloading LCPVs at Massacre Bay, May 13, 1943. The narrow beach hemmed in by steep mountains is apparent, and a serious logistic logjam developed here. Supplies had to be brought to the front by hand, and Brown's Attu Landing Force proved short of necessary manpower. (Naval History and Heritage Command)

A severe Japanese counterattack was eventually repulsed through hand-to-hand fighting late that night. Hartl had lost 14 killed, 15 wounded, and 12 evacuated due to exposure. Japanese casualties were 90 killed and wounded.

Led by Captain Toshio Hayashi's 1st Company/303rd, the main Japanese positions in the south looked down from heights above the center of Massacre Valley and over Jarmin Pass. By May 12, Hayashi's 200 infantry and mountain artillery battery had decisively halted Southern Force's advance. Japanese fire had killed Colonel Earle while he and an Alaska Scout were on a dangerous reconnaissance mission; Brown replaced Earle with his own chief of staff, Colonel Wayne Zimmerman. Brown and his deputy, chief of artillery Brigadier-General Archibald Arnold, then personally scouted the Massacre Valley front lines. By 1140hrs, *Perida* had begun landing BCT 32-2 at Massacre Bay, but Aleutian static drowned unheard Brown's three separate requests to land reserve BCTs 32-1 and 32-3. *Perida* then rammed an underwater pinnacle and began to flood; she duly ran herself aground to effect repairs.

By May 13, Brown's assault transports were still only half unloaded. Northern Force's logistic operation at Holtz Bay under beachmaster Commander "Squeaky" Anderson proceeded smoothly, but at Massacre Bay a complete breakdown in the inland supply train meant a massive supply jam back at the beach. Unneeded anti-aircraft units were cannibalized for manual labor, and large numbers of combat troops were drawn out of the lines to hand-carry supplies. Officers were forced to give ammunition priority, leaving freezing front-line troops without even sleeping bags.

Attu had immediately revealed itself a defender's paradise. Lacking maps of Attu's interior, Brown's infantry were typically channeled through valleys and draws, which were surrounded by higher, steeper ground ahead and on both sides. Solid fog banks crouched halfway up the mountains but left the valley floors clear, hiding entrenched Japanese positions above but leaving the Americans below visible to the Japanese. Enjoying interior lines of communication, Japanese entrenchments, invisible in the mist, were arranged in open horseshoes that enveloped US advances in three-sided firing sacks. Flanking maneuvers in the steep mountain valleys were virtually impossible, requiring uphill advances into the teeth of Japanese fire, described as "like attacking a pillbox by way of a tightrope." Steep escarpments demanded US heavy weapons be rope-hauled up sheer cliffs to advance. If Japanese positions appeared on the verge of collapse, Japanese defenders melted into the fog and re-established new defensive lines shortly behind, having given up few casualties and little ground. Small Japanese detachments were thus able to frustrate larger US forces, which could not even find their enemy. Meanwhile, occupying soggy foxholes, criminally under-clothed US troops began succumbing en masse to frostbite, trench foot, and hypothermia.

On May 13, Southern Force reached within 200 yards of Jarmin Pass before Hayashi's 1st Company/303rd repulsed them. Meanwhile, Rockwell finally received Brown's urgent requests for BCTs 32-1 and 32-3. At Massacre Bay, BCT 32-1 debarked USS *U. S. Grant* without incident to reinforce Southern Force. In the north, however, USAT *Chirikof* attempted several landing approaches but was driven back each time by intense Japanese fire. Concentrated TF-51 naval fire and strafing *Nassau* Wildcats finally suppressed Japanese artillery long enough to allow *Chirikof* to approach; by 1730hrs, *Chirikof* was landing Lieutenant-Colonel John "Mickey" Finn's BCT 32-3 at Beach Red. Brown then requested *Landcrab*'s final reserves, Buckner's BCT 4-1 at Adak, which Rockwell denied due to the already-congested beaches. By nightfall May 13, Brown, in only intermittent contact with his northern troops, reported US casualties as 44 killed, 74 missing, and 171 wounded.

US troops advance up an Attu hill on May 13, 1943. The coastal Attu fog will shortly envelop them. Aleutian weather was not actually Arctic, but rather an especially snowy variant of the oceanic climate common to the Pacific Northwest and Northwest Europe. (Naval History and Heritage Command)

The following day, May 14, Brown's Southern Force resumed its futile frontal assaults up Massacre Valley. After a particularly urgent close air support call, *Nassau* launched eight fighters in poor weather. A sudden williwaw smashed two Wildcats into the Massacre Valley floor. A third was shot down over Jarmin Pass, while a fourth crashed returning to *Nassau*.

However, Northern Force's creeping advance imperiled Yamasaki's Holtz Bay defenders. The morning of May 14, Yamasaki reluctantly ordered a fighting withdrawal east toward Fishhook Ridge and Clevesy Pass. Corporal Asatake recalled, "The reversal in fortune led to a feeling of defeat for the army that remained." By evening May 14, Yamasaki's casualties were 59 killed and 64 wounded. Evacuating Japanese troops "walked in like gaunt ghosts" from their outlying posts the night of May 14/15, most having survived on one cold rice ball a day since May 11. As Tokyo broadcast florid praise and imperial exhortations to Attu's garrison, Yamasaki ordered his Holtz Bay headquarters to burn documents and prepare to kill Japanese too wounded to evacuate.

Among Attu's Japanese garrison was 31-year-old Sergeant-Major Paul Nobuo Tatsuguchi, a California-trained IJA physician and devout Seventh Day Adventist, described by his widow as "a faithful Christian doctor and gentleman who devoted himself to God and communities." Tatsuguchi's captured diary would become an American public sensation when translated and published after the battle. Tatsuguchi marveled at the fierceness of US air and sea bombardments, while casually recording, "The enemy has a great number of Negroes and Indians." Observing from Holtz Bay, Tatsuguchi noted, "Facial expressions back from West Arm [are] tense. [Before long] they all went back to the firing line..."

In the north, unable to raise radio contact, Willoughby's isolated Scouts continued inching forward while stubbornly fighting off Japanese troops who hurled epithets in English: "Damn American dogs, we massacre you!" Retreat was impossible – food was exhausted, ammunition nearly spent, and half of Willoughby's men were combat or exposure casualties. Nevertheless, the Scouts' ferocious resistance convinced at least some Japanese they were fighting a division. That night, the Scouts again dug in. Willoughby claimed, "Since we couldn't sleep at night, we weren't about to let the enemy sleep. We kept up a din around the clock so that the enemy couldn't divert any

Six combat troops are seen evacuating a single casualty to the rear on Attu. Alaska veterans assigned to the ad hoc committee to help train the US 7th Division in California complained bitterly that their advice was not being heeded. Among the most important was the knowledge that vehicles were completely worthless on Aleutian muskeg and would have to be compensated for with excessive manpower. (Bettmann via Getty Images)

forces away from us to Culin." However, the Japanese would withdraw overnight.

The following morning, May 15, 80 of Willoughby's Scouts occupied the abandoned Japanese positions. At 1100hrs, Culin's Northern Force of BCT 17-1 and BCT 32-3 took Yamasaki's hastily abandoned headquarters at Holtz Bay's West Arm. By 1530hrs, having gone four days without food or sleep, the remaining 230 Scouts rendezvoused with Northern Force. Many Scouts were feverish and vomiting on empty stomachs because of cold, exposure, and hunger. They had suffered 11 KIA (including Captain Austin) and 20 combat wounded. Only 40 could still walk, the rest crawling on bloody knees and feet. Rampant frostbite and gangrene claimed scores of fingers, toes, and feet to amputation. After recuperating, some 150 Scouts would volunteer for further duty by May 18.

Offshore, multiple four-torpedo spreads just missed transport *J. Franklin Bell* and battleship *Pennsylvania*, while six P-38 Lightnings dropped parafrag bombs on Holtz Bay and strafed Japanese positions. Japanese personnel not participating in immediate combat attempted to hide by day and move by night; Tatsuguchi recorded a Lightning "spat fire and flew past our cave."

At the Massacre Valley front, Colonel Zimmerman had replaced the heavily battered BCT 17-3 with BCT 32-2 the night of May 14/15. On May 15 (and again on May 16), BCT 32-2 would attack up Massacre Valley and be repulsed. Meanwhile, an angry Brown departed Beach Yellow the afternoon of May 15 to personally confer with Rockwell aboard *Pennsylvania*. Afterwards a converted, sympathetic Rockwell forwarded Brown's request for Buckner's BCT 4-1, but also attached a long, unexplained request for 60 days' heavy road-building equipment.

Brown and his superior Kinkaid had never actually met in person. Equally frustrated, both had fired numerous unanswered transmissions back and forth since D-Day – Brown pleading for reinforcements and Kinkaid demanding situation reports. Kinkaid now found himself aghast at this latest request. Requests to clarify again went unanswered. Convinced Brown had resigned himself to stalemate, Kinkaid conferred with Buckner, DeWitt, and Nimitz. On May 16, over an angry Rockwell's objections, Kinkaid relieved Brown as Attu Force commander, appointing Alaska veteran Brigadier-General Eugene Landrum as Brown's replacement.

Departing Adak, Brigadier-General Landrum arrived at Attu the afternoon of May 16 and took command at 1700hrs. After reviewing the situation with Brown, Landrum absolved Brown of fault, announced Brown's Attu plan was basically sound and would remain unaltered, and announced he had no intention of stealing credit from Brown or his men. Brown then made his Attu exit.

Ordered by Kinkaid, Colonel Eareckson commenced reporting directly to Landrum that evening and exchanged his Amchitka-based B-24 Liberator for a *Casco*-based OS2U Kingfisher. Eareckson, orbiting relentlessly overhead every day despite the appalling weather, now directly commanded Attu airspace. With transports fully unloaded on May 16, Kinkaid ordered Rockwell's TF-51 to withdraw, leaving gunboat *Charleston*, destroyer *Phelps*, and tender *Casco* under Landrum's direct command. Escort carrier *Nassau* retired having lost seven aircraft in 86 combat sorties. TF-16 remained to offer logistic support and continue the Attu blockade.

A fresh-looking US infantry column snakes up a hillside at Attu, May 1942. They are likely reinforcements or relief to front-line units. Many of the Aleutian campaign's excellent color photos are due to contemporary *Life* magazine articles. (Dmitri Kessel/The LIFE Premium Collection/ Getty Images)

Above Holtz Bay the Japanese were in full retreat. That evening, Tatsuguchi would find himself getting lost in the fog, collapsing every 20–30 steps, falling asleep in the snow, dreaming, and waking up again multiple times as he retreated in delirium toward Chichagof Harbor. By the late evening of May 16, Culin's Northern Force had pushed to the base of Moore Ridge separating the West and East Arms of Holtz Bay. Northern Force was now in the rear of the Japanese defending Massacre Valley against Southern Force. After repelling five major attacks from Zimmerman's Southern Force, tactical reality forced Yamasaki to withdraw Captain Hayashi's undefeated but dangerously exposed 1st Company/303rd from Jarmin Pass toward Chichagof Harbor.

At 0010hrs, May 17, Culin's Northern Force unleashed an aggressive night attack on Moore Ridge, and by 0300hrs, Culin realized Moore Ridge had already been abandoned. Hours later, patrols discovered the Japanese had evacuated entirely, and all of Holtz Bay was in American hands. Meanwhile, Southern Force's Colonel Zimmerman suspected Jarmin Pass had also been evacuated. After a personal reconnaissance, Zimmerman sent advance patrols ahead. They summited Jarmin Pass and linked up with Culin's Northern Force in the early dark of May 18. It was the moment Yamasaki's men had tenaciously struggled to prevent since D-Day. The final destruction of Japan's Attu garrison was now a matter of time and casualties.

The drive against Chichagof Harbor, May 19–28

Landrum used May 18 to rest and reorganize American forces before the final push toward Chichagof Harbor – *Landcrab*'s endgame. With only three of the original 93 US landing craft still serviceable, the logistic operation remained difficult. While waiting for Adak tugs and barges to arrive, ship-to-shore supply was improvised through PT boats, captured Daihatsu barges, and taxiing PBYs.

On May 19, Landrum's recombined Attu Force began methodically advancing toward Yamasaki's final redoubt at Chichagof Harbor, just four miles east. The battle resumed its brutal straight-ahead character of previous days; Landrum, however, crucially chose to first conquer the surrounding ridges' high crests before occupying low ground. Yamasaki had again skillfully deployed his defense; Japanese troops even fired from cracks in the rocks. Landrum countered by dragging 37mm guns up the passes and blasting tight positions with high-explosive rounds.

US troops of an all-black labor battalion eating at Attu's Massacre Bay, March 20, 1943. Suicide rates among US personnel assigned to Alaska were categorically higher than the wartime average. Blacks, disproportionately drawn from the warm, sunny American South, suffered the highest rate. (World War II Database)

Hartl's BCT 17-1 began consolidating the Holtz Bay area against anticipated Japanese counter-landings on May 19. After a reinforced company climbing the steep Prendergast Ridge was repulsed by Japanese snipers and machine-gun fire, all of BCT 17-1 was committed; they would not clear Prendergast Ridge and reach the imposing snow-covered Fishhook Ridge until May 25. At 0952hrs, BCT 17-2 attacked Clevesy Pass; by afternoon, BCT 32-2 had conquered the high ground to the northeast, but was stubbornly resisted by a heavily entrenched Japanese platoon at 2,000ft Point Able.

By May 20, transport *St Mihiel* had landed BCT 4-1 at Massacre Bay. BCT 4-1 marched to the front, relieved BCT 17-1, and eventually cleared Clevesy Pass. The following day, May 21, BCT 32-2 resumed its attack on Lieutenant Honna's high ground at Point Able. Meanwhile, USAAF B-25s and P-38s destroyed what remained of Chichagof Harbor's old Aleut village. Newly arrived to observe his BCT 4-1, Buckner joined Eareckson and Castner on an aerial tour of the battlefield, strafing Japanese positions with the Kingfisher's tail-mounted .30-caliber machine gun. When poor weather grounded them, Eareckson grabbed a rifle and hiked to Point Able for a first-hand view of the fighting. After a Japanese sniper grazed his back, Eareckson shot his assailant dead, then returned to Massacre Bay. A waiting Buckner pinned a Purple Heart on Eareckson, then sarcastically kicked Eareckson's backside, "for being where you had no business being." That evening BCT 32-2's Company E won Point Able in an uphill charge, exterminating Lieutenant Honna's 2nd Company/303rd in the process.

IGHQ's response to *Landcrab* had been disorganized and uninspired – *Landcrab* had come a month earlier than expected. Higuchi's Operation Order No. 19 had immediately directed ten days' rations be parachuted to Attu and ordered the Asahikawa Division to prepare a 4,700-strong counter-landing. However, Kawase's May 12 sortie with heavy cruiser *Maya* and destroyer *Usugumo* had quickly aborted upon learning the size of TF-51, returning to Paramushiro on May 15. Weather also aborted a May 13 attack by 20 Paramushiro-based G4M bombers and had grounded them since. Within days, Yamasaki was reporting 10,000 US troops ashore at Attu. At Sapporo, Fifth Fleet's feeble strength was finally revealed to a "thunderstruck" Higuchi. In response, the IJN authorized Operation *Kita* (*North*). Sortieing from Truk for Tokyo Bay on May 16, Admiral Mineichi Koga would command carriers *Shokaku*, *Zuikaku*, *Hiyo*, and *Junyo* (240 aircraft), battleships *Musashi*, *Kongo*, and *Haruna*, five heavy cruisers, two light cruisers, and 16 destroyers to crush the US blockade. However, IGHQ canceled Operation Order No. 19 on May 19, suspended *Kita* "to await developments" upon Koga's May 21 arrival, and simultaneously ordered Operation *KE*, the evacuation of Kiska. Nevertheless, Japanese radio continued broadcasting Yamasaki's men tales of naval victories and promises of rescue just days away.

By late May 21, all of Clevesy Pass and its surrounding heights of Cold Mountain, Engineer Hill, and Point Able were under American control.

Meanwhile, Talley's engineers were frantically working to build roads so heavy equipment could be brought closer to the front. Covered by three heavy weapons companies, BCT 17-3 opened its assault on the Sarana Nose promontory at 0640hrs, May 22. A heavy pre-attack bombardment so badly shook Japanese defenders that by afternoon a well-coordinated infantry–artillery assault took Sarana Nose with unusually light casualties. In dense fog, similarly crushing artillery fire eventually allowed BCT 4-1 to more painfully conquer the crest of Prendergast Ridge from Prendergast's southern slope.

Twin-engined IJN bombers overfly the snowy Aleutians in an undated wartime photo. These appear to be G3M Nells rather than the G4M Bettys reported on May 23, 1943. The snow cover however is consistent with that day's freshly fallen heavy snowfall. Regardless, most of the day's IJN bombers failed to make it back to Paramushiro. (World War II Database)

That afternoon, at 1548hrs, gunboat *Charleston* and destroyer *Phelps* just evaded torpedoes from 15 G4M bombers that snuck undetected into Holtz Bay. American anti-aircraft fire shot down two Bettys and exploded a torpedo in mid-air. Surviving G4Ms flew inland, dropped supply packages, and retired. The following day, a 19-plane G4M strike from Paramushiro was detected 70 miles out by the radar-equipped US destroyer picket, then sighted over Attu by a Catalina. A patrol of five P-38 Lightnings shot down 12 G4Ms; survivors dumped their bombs harmlessly and fled. Only seven Bettys returned to Paramushiro; the Americans lost two P-38s.

May 23 brought a day-long snowfall. BCT 17-2 relieved BCT 4-1 that morning. Rather than advance up the low-lying Chichagof Valley toward Chichagof Harbor, Landrum chose to first capture the icy, jagged Fishhook Ridge looming above to the north. A coordinated 1000hrs, May 24 attack between Northern Force's BCT 32-3 and Southern Force's BCT 17-2 was ultimately repelled by heavy Japanese fire. The night of May 24/25, an American anti-aircraft battery fought through heavy snowfall to valiantly manhandle two 75mm pack howitzers from Moore Ridge to Prendergast Ridge, providing critical fire support to the Fishhook drive. The following morning, Company E, 17th RCT penetrated a deep, snow-covered, 200-yard Japanese trench on the Fishhook that had pinned BCT 32-3.

As Yamasaki's Chichagof Harbor perimeter shrank ever smaller, American bombardments increased to hellish intensity. Remorseless US artillery smashed Japanese facilities, killing defenders via shrapnel, debris, and cave-ins. Tatsuguchi lived in a resigned daze:

> It felt like the Misumi Barracks had blown up and everything was [shaken] up tremendously. Consciousness became vague. One tent burned down from [an] incendiary bomb. Strafing planes hit the next room. Two hits from .50-caliber shell. My room looks an awful mess ... The last line of Umanose [Fishhook] was broken through. No hope for reinforcements, will die for the cause of the Imperial Edict.

By dawn, May 26, BCT 17-2 and BCT 4-1's Company B held the Fishhook's base, then covered two BCT 4-1 platoons wiping out the remaining Fishhook trench from above. Brutal small-unit actions erupted among the steep, jagged peaks of the eastern Fishhook between BCT 4-1 and Japanese defenders. From the north, BCT 32-3 and BCT 17-1 conquered the northern slope of the Fishhook, at times assaulting 60-degree inclines. Rallying his stalled comrades in the face of severe heavy weapons fire, 19-year-old Private Joe P. Martínez charged a steep ridge and single-handedly destroyed multiple

Japanese positions in succession; he was mortally wounded attacking the final trench at the summit. Martínez was posthumously awarded Attu's only Medal of Honor.

A US 105mm howitzer is seen bombarding Japanese positions at Attu. The steep cliffs, hovering fog bank, and lack of sufficient cold-weather clothing are once again noteworthy. Superior artillery proved a major US advantage during Operation *Landcrab*. (US Navy/Frederic Lewis/ Getty Images)

Unusually clear weather brought a 62-plane US airstrike on Chichagof Harbor. Tatsuguchi confided, "less than 1,000 [Japanese are] left from more than 2,000 troops." Wracked with pain and diarrhea, Tatsuguchi "took everything from pills, opium, [and] morphine, then slept pretty well." Strafing US fighters destroyed his roof.

Once the Fishhook was taken, only the lower Buffalo Ridge would remain between the Americans and Yamasaki's final Chichagof Harbor redoubt. With the Fishhook battle still underway, BCTs 32-1 and 32-2 attacked the low ground preceding Buffalo Ridge on May 27. Corporal Asatake admitted to himself, "It cannot end in our favor, we are defeated ... I find myself thinking these thoughts often." Tatsuguchi's entry was equally grim:

> The remaining rations are for only two days. Our artillery has been completely destroyed ... The companies on the bottom of Attu-Fuji have been completely annihilated except one ... Other companies have been completely annihilated except one or two ... Continuous cases of suicide. Half of sector unit headquarters was blown away ... [Ate] half-fried thistle. It is the first time I have eaten something fresh in six months.

By May 28, Landrum's troops had conquered the Fishhook, and at 1830hrs, BCTs 32-1 and 32-2 assaulted a Buffalo Ridge softened up by overwhelming US artillery. By nightfall, the Americans had taken part of the Buffalo Ridge crest and were looking down into Chichagof Harbor.

Yamasaki's starving Attu garrison was clearly doomed. IGHQ officially canceled Operation *Kita* on May 28 and recalled a preposterous May 24 mission by *Kiso*, *Abukuma*, and four destroyers to ground themselves in Chichagof Harbor; they had never approached within 150 miles of Attu. Kawase additionally reported a final desperate attempt to evacuate select officers by submarine had been repelled by US destroyers.

On Attu the end grew near. Just 800 able-bodied and 600 grievously wounded Japanese remained against Yamasaki's estimate of 14,000 Americans. A resigned Higuchi informed Yamasaki no option remained except a glorious sacrifice. Yamasaki responded that he would "implement [such] based on Higuchi-san's intentions," claiming he had no regrets and would "hit the Americans with one final charge. We shall live forever and pray for the glory of the homeland. Banzai to the Emperor." Yamasaki's forlorn objective was to break into the American rear, turn US artillery on Massacre Valley, plunder supplies, and live in the Attu hinterlands until an unlikely rescue.

That day, May 28, after an entire grueling battle fought uphill, Landrum began marshalling Attu Force for the following morning's coup de grace – an overwhelming downhill charge into Chichagof Harbor. Though backed against the Bering Sea, Yamasaki's men nevertheless met American calls to surrender with silent *mokusatsu* – "scornful contempt."

Attu's Chichagof Harbor seen, with Japanese positions burning from a recent US air attack, May 1943. With the odds severely against them, the surviving Japanese were pushed back to where their occupation began 12 months earlier. Chichagof Harbor's Aleut village was never rebuilt. (Library of Congress, LC-USW33-029017-ZC)

Tatsuguchi's final entry hours before Yamasaki's banzai charge follows in its entirety:

> May 28, 1943 – Battle …
>
> Today at 2000hrs we assembled in front of headquarters. The field hospital took part too. The last assault is to be carried out; all the patients in the hospital were to commit suicide. Only 31 years of living and I am to die here. I have no regrets. Banzai to the Emperor. I am grateful that I have kept the peace in my soul which Christ bestowed upon me. At 1800hrs took care of all the patients with grenades. Good-bye Taeki my beloved wife, who loved me to the last, until we meet again, I greet you Godspeed. I feel sorry for you Takiko, born February of this year and gone without seeing your father – Hisaka, who just turned four years old, will grow up unhindered. Well, be good. Matsuo (brother) Kochan, Sakeghan, Massachan, Mittichan, good-bye.
>
> The number participating in the attack is a little over 1,000, to take enemy artillery positions. It seems the enemy is expecting an all-out attack tomorrow … end …

Yamasaki's banzai charge, May 29

Leading from the front ranks, Yamasaki unleashed his surprise midnight counterattack at 0030hrs, May 29. Roughly 800 Japanese troops flowed silently up lightly defended Chichagof Valley, bypassing the main front-line US strength on the ridges above. At Lake Cories, BCT 32-1's Company B had been ordered to evacuate to the battalion field kitchen for a pre-assault breakfast. Armed with bayonets, swords, and grenades, "a thousand howling Japanese" slammed into Company B's unsuspecting rearguard at 0330hrs. Organized resistance was impossible and the panic-stricken Company B fled in front of the Japanese or scrambled up adjacent slopes. Yamasaki's men overran two US command posts and a field hospital in Sarana Valley where they bayoneted American wounded. Surviving Americans played dead for 36 hours while yards away starving Japanese frantically pilfered American food, cigarettes, and weapons.

However, Yamasaki's counterattack progressively lost strength as it streamed west because Japanese troops dispersed to attack strong US positions

BANZAI CHARGE AT ATTU'S ENGINEER HILL, 0500HRS, MAY 29, 1943 (PP. 82–83)

Although the Americans met and ultimately repulsed Yamasaki's surprise banzai charge with varying degrees of success throughout the adjacent Chichagof Valley, the most decisive and arguably most dramatic location was at Engineer Hill, a low, insignificant rise in the valley, surrounded by Attu's high, steep mountains. Estimated at a total of 600 men, the screaming Japanese charge slammed into Engineer Hill at 0500hrs, May 29.

Able-bodied Japanese troops that had survived to May 29 were typically suffering from poor health and previous wounds. Low on ammunition, many troops brandished swords, empty rifles, makeshift spears, and stolen US weapons. Waving his sword, Yamasaki is seen here at the center front of the Japanese charge (**1**), just as he had laid out hours earlier in his 14-part attack instructions preceding the charge. Between the night's utter chaos and Attu's extremely few Japanese survivors, it is fair to imagine Yamasaki's exact fate. It is plausible that Yamasaki died in the front lines early at Engineer Hill, sword in hand.

The US rear positions were unusually vulnerable that morning. The day before, preparing for May 29's planned final Chichagof Harbor assault, Landrum had pulled all combat reserves to the front lines. While many US support troops resisted at Engineer Hill, a substantial portion were from the 50th Combat Engineer Battalion, whom the hill and battle are named after. Brigadier-General Archibald Arnold (**2**), 7th Division artillery chief and deputy commander, coolly organized a hasty defense centered on the high ground of Engineer Hill. Using hand-signals, Arnold directed grenade throws into the successive Japanese waves. As support troops surprised in the middle of the night, the Americans had to scramble for small arms and not everyone was armed. The Americans shortly manhandled a 37mm M3 anti-tank gun to Engineer Hill's crest, the improvised US defense position's only heavy weapon.

There was no single decisive moment when the Japanese attack was broken. Rather, over the course of several hours, successive Japanese waves assaulted the Engineer Hill crest and were repeatedly driven back, often temporarily retreating into the valley to reorganize and rally for another attack. With strengthening daylight, having realized the attack had failed, Japanese survivors melted back into Attu's hinterlands. The 50th Engineers claimed 350 enemy killed at a loss of 17 dead and 35 wounded. The Americans estimated over half the Japanese attackers survived the actual banzai charge and most committed suicide in the following days.

Dead Japanese soldiers seen in Chichagof Valley after the final, unsuccessful banzai charge. Several hundred Japanese bodies were never found by US authorities. These missing Japanese were presumably buried by their comrades during the battle, buried by American bombardments, or died in caves after committing suicide. (World War II Database)

at Sarana Nose and surrounding areas. Surprised Americans suffered casualties but ultimately repelled these subsidiary Japanese attacks. Thus dissipated, the weakened main Japanese force finally collided with US support personnel at Clevesy Pass and Engineer Hill at 0500hrs. Yamasaki's men had advanced 2.5 miles. Panic-stricken Americans ran past US reserve positions, screaming hysterically, "The Japs are coming!" Under the composed direction of Brigadier-General Archibald Arnold, scrambling troops of the 50th Combat Engineer Battalion and other support units formed a hastily improvised defense line as the main weight of the fanatical assault hit them.

From the base of Engineer Hill, the banzai-screaming Japanese mob repeatedly charged uphill toward the US reserves and in hand-to-hand combat the Americans frantically repulsed them each time. Gradually, the desperate Americans recovered their wits and reinforcements steadily streamed in. A small Japanese band broke through Clevesy Pass and reached the Hogback in Massacre Valley. They were stopped just short of a 105mm battery – Yamasaki's original goal. Desperate fighting continued with daylight.

By a frighteningly slim margin Yamasaki's breath-taking gamble had failed. Most of May 29 and May 30 saw the Americans recovering lost ground, rescuing trapped US survivors, and hunting down the remaining Japanese, many of whom committed suicide. US troops captured Chichagof Harbor against minimal organized resistance the afternoon of May 30. Attu was declared secure, although isolated survivors would hold out until September 8. Attu had been an old-style infantry–artillery battle of trenches and frontal assaults, supposedly obsolete in 1943. US artillery had expended 32,270 105mm rounds and over 10,000 75mm shells. US officials counted 2,351 Japanese bodies. Just 28 Japanese were captured alive, none of them officers. Of Attu's 3,829 American casualties, 549 were KIA and 1,148 wounded in action. Some 1,200 wounded were cold-weather related, primarily frostbite and trench foot. Another 932 casualties were due to disease and accidents. Many Americans suffered permanent injuries from the cold, including numerous cases of both feet requiring amputation. As a percentage of the attacking force, Attu would prove the United States' second-costliest Pacific War island battle after Iwo Jima.

THE LIBERATION OF KISKA, AUGUST 1943

Attu's fall extracted a rare upbraiding from the Emperor himself; on June 6–7, Hirohito personally excoriated IJA and IJN officials for failing to hold or successfully resupply the island, pleading, "Isn't there some way, some place, where we can win a real victory over the Americans?" With Attu taken, the Americans' Kiska blockade clinched tighter. US engineers quickly began construction of two Attu airstrips; the first was operational on June 9. Additionally, on May 30, Brigadier-General John Copeland's 2,500 troops and engineers had landed at nearby Shemya to build a 10,000ft airstrip for B-29 Superfortresses; this airstrip was landing fighters by June 21.

Kawase had already commenced his desperate submarine evacuation of Kiska. But on June 10, 675-ton sub-chaser USS *PC-487* rammed and sank 5,000-ton *I-24* off Shemya, followed three days later by destroyer USS *Frazier*'s destruction of *I-31*. Destroyer USS *Monaghan* then chased *I-7* aground at Kiska the night of June 22/23. All three I-boats had been carrying Kiska evacuees. Kawase had thus far embarked 820 troops, but had lost 300 of them to the US blockade. Having lost three submarines, Kawase scuttled the submarine evacuation for a bolder plan.

Meanwhile, Kinkaid and Butler continued to pummel Kiska. Four cruisers and five destroyers shelled Kiska on July 6, while USAAF bombers joined two battleships, five cruisers, and nine destroyers to pound Kiska in clear weather on July 22. The bombardment produced extensive damage but only 15 Japanese dead and 13 wounded, thanks to heavy subterranean shelters.

By now US forces had begun attacking the Kuriles themselves. On July 15, submarine USS *Narwhal* had shelled the Kuriles' Matsuwa Airfield, and on July 18, six B-24s bombed Paramushiro's airstrip and harbor, successfully outrunning five pursuing Zeroes. Nine B-24s would bomb Paramushiro again on August 10, losing one B-24 to a combination of flak and the alerted Japanese fighters.

The Battle of the Pips and the evacuation of Kiska, July 26–28

Eighty miles south of Kiska, at 0045hrs, July 26, battleship *Mississippi*'s SC radar detected seven targets 15 miles to the northeast, proceeding at 16 knots – independently triangulated by radars aboard battleship *New Mexico* and cruisers *Portland* and *Wichita*. TG-16.22 closed to 24,000 yards and at 0113hrs, Rear Admiral Robert Giffen ordered all ships with radar contact to open fire. For 67 minutes *Mississippi*, *New Mexico*, and cruisers *Portland*, *Wichita*, and *Louisville* discharged their main batteries into the radar contacts. *Mississippi*'s log recorded zigzags and a 20-degree course change. Cruisers *San Francisco* and *Santa Fe* registered shell splashes, but never the alleged targets. Seventy-five miles away at Kiska, Japanese sentries were treated to a spectacular night-time lightshow on the horizon.

By 0222hrs, TG-16.22's radar contacts had faded out and Giffen ceased fire. No wreckage or flotsam was ever found – thousands of American shells had seemingly unloaded into empty ocean. Numerous unconvincing arguments have been

Seaplane tender USS *Gillis* (AVD-12) and three 78ft Higgins PT boats of MTBRon-13 seen in Attu's Casco Cove, Massacre Bay, June 1943. PT boats made arduous sea crossings to reach the Aleutians but proved unsuccessful there. *Gillis* was converted from a Clemson-class destroyer in 1940 and supported the June 1942 Kiska Blitz. (NavSource.org)

Operation *Cottage*, August 15–18

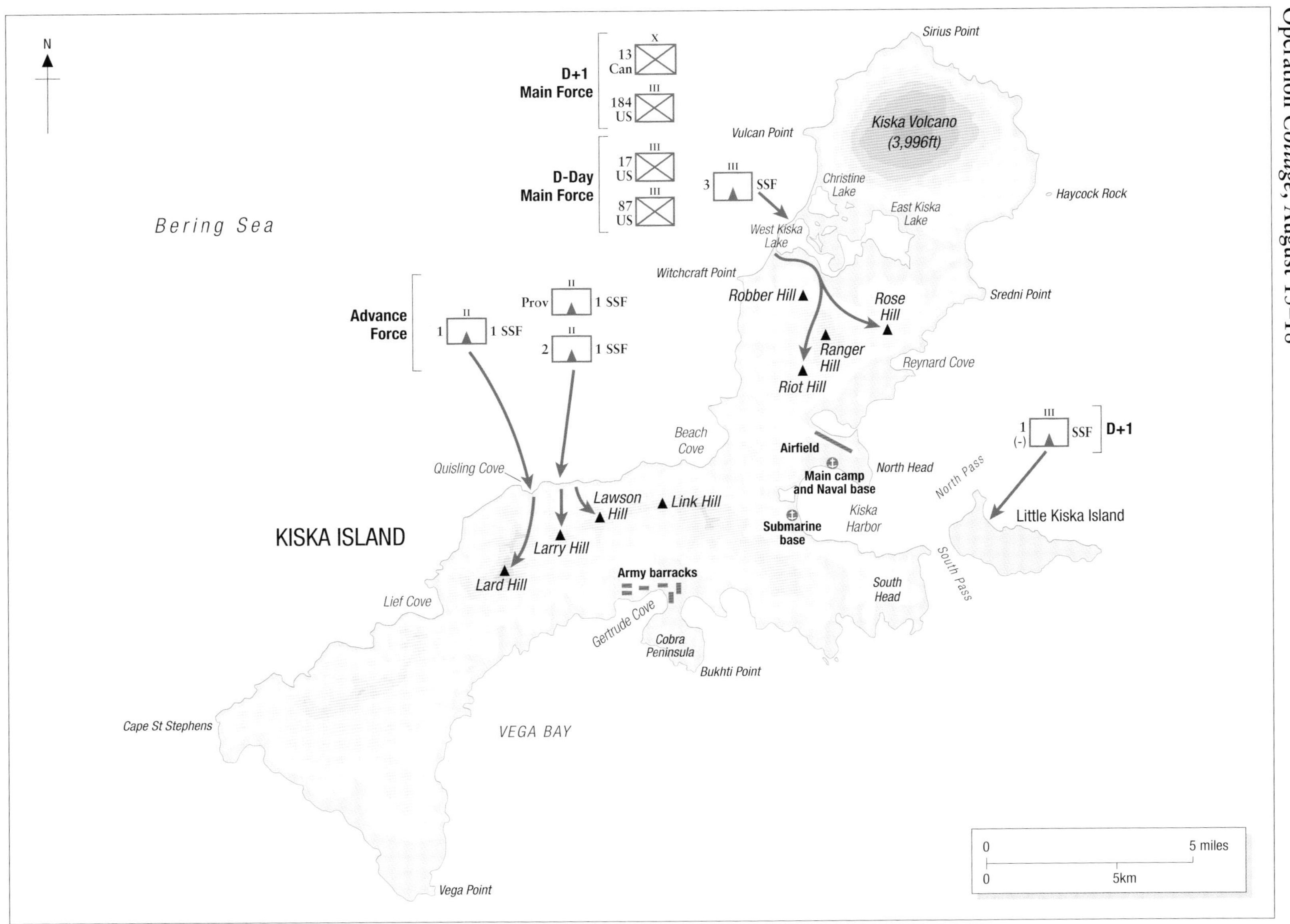

forwarded to explain "The Battle of the Pips," including the US Navy's official conclusion blaming the echoes on atmospheric phenomena. Eleven IJN submarines were in the North Pacific but no hard evidence exists as to whether any were ever under attack. What actually happened that night remains one of World War II's enduring minor mysteries.

Regardless, the "Pips" incident required TG-16.22 to leave its Kiska station to replenish; simultaneously, a snowstorm ruined Kinkaid's PT-boat blockade. Recognizing his opening, Kawase, in light cruiser *Tama*, initiated a desperate but highly choreographed surface rescue mission. Sneaking through fog, Rear Admiral Masatomi Kimura's light cruisers *Kiso* and *Abukuma* and nine destroyers dropped anchor in Kiska Harbor at 1835hrs, July 28. Evacuating Japanese troops threw their rifles into the sea, boarded 39 barges, and clambered up rope ladders. At 1930hrs, Kimura's flotilla rejoined *Tama* and sped homeward at 30 knots, having embarked all 5,183 men in 55 minutes. By August 1, they were safely back in Paramushiro.

Operation *Cottage*, August 15–16, 1943

US intelligence had estimated 10,000 Japanese on Kiska. The JCS authorized overwhelming power for Kiska's Operation *Cottage* – 34,426 well-prepared Allied troops under US Major-General Charles Corlett, including the 5,300 Canadians of "Greenlight Force." Air strength comprised 108 bombers and 60 fighters; Rockwell's naval strength entailed battleships *Pennsylvania*, *Idaho*, and *Tennessee*, two cruisers, 19 destroyers, 20 transports and freighters, 14 LSTs, nine LCI(L)s, 19 LCT(5)s, and nine auxiliaries.

On July 30, Operation *Cottage* was approved; D-Day was set for August 15. However, US intelligence began receiving disconcerting evidence Kiska had been evacuated – radio silence and photo-reconnaissance indicated an empty island. Nevertheless, intermittent flak reports frustrated the consensus. A plausible explanation held the Japanese had retreated to Kiska's fog-shrouded higher-elevations, as they had at Attu. Yet so convinced were most USAAF pilots that Kiska was abandoned that in early August, Captain George Ruddell's flight of P-40s landed at Kiska and walked about taking photos for an hour, completely without orders. However, Kinkaid ultimately vetoed landing an official reconnaissance party, reasoning that invading even an empty Kiska provided a "super dress rehearsal, good for training purposes."

Landing Force Kiska – Major-General Charles Corlett

- 7th Infantry Division (US)
    - 17th Infantry Regiment
    - 53rd Infantry Regiment
    - 184th Infantry Regiment
- 4th Infantry Regiment (US)
- 87th Mountain Infantry Regiment (US)
- 1st Special Service Force Brigade (US–Canadian)
- Greenlight Force (Canadian)
    - 13th Canadian Infantry Brigade Group, 6th Canadian Infantry Division
        - Canadian Fusiliers (City of London) Regiment
        - Winnipeg Grenadiers, First Battalion
        - Rocky Mountain Rangers Regiment
        - Le Régiment de Hull

Mountainous, fog-bound Kiska is 22 miles long and 3–4 miles wide, reaching 3,996ft at Kiska Volcano in its far northeast. Kiska's primary inlets are at Kiska Harbor and Gertrude Cove. D-Day fog rendered aerial reconnaissance impossible. After naval bombardments and demonstration feints, 1st Regiment, 1st Special Service Force reconnoitered northern Kiska at 0110hrs, August 15. Landing behind them were the US 17th Regimental Combat Team and US 87th Mountain Infantry Regiment. The US 184th Regimental Combat Team and 13th Canadian Infantry Brigade Group would land on D+1. However, D-Day landings revealed heavy evidence that Kiska was abandoned. Gertrude Cove, assumed to be heavily fortified, was also empty. August 16's pre-arranged naval fire proceeded, but with ammunition allowances halved.

Icy rain and disorienting fog shortly reduced visibility to zero. Sporadic small-arms fire reverberated throughout Kiska, producing eerie glowing flashes. Rumors abounded of firefights and Allied casualties. Japanese mines and booby traps added to the bewilderment. Climbing uphill, Japanese fortifications were always found empty. Allied troops, investigating Kiska dugouts, found only half-eaten meals and mocking graffiti. Above ground were piles of abandoned, sabotaged heavy weapons and extensive wreckage, including A6M-2N Rufes and midget submarines – and the original USN weather team's dog Explosion, abandoned but still alive. On August 17, Rockwell released *Tennessee*, *Idaho*, and their destroyers to *Adak*, and began re-embarking heavy equipment.

The reports of firefights had been true – but had been Allied troops shooting at each other through the mist. Total Allied ground casualties were 22 killed and 174 wounded, of whom 14 killed and almost 170 wounded were due to friendly fire; the remainder fell to Japanese booby traps. The Americans suffered 18 killed and 170 wounded, the Canadians four killed and four wounded. The following day, August 18, destroyer USS *Abner Read* struck a Japanese mine in Kiska Harbor, killing 70 and wounding 47. *Abner Read* brought total *Cottage* casualties to 313 (92 killed, 221 wounded). With the Japanese long gone, *Cottage* had proved an expensive embarrassment. Corlett admittedly was "tickled pink we didn't have to fight." Kinkaid mused, "Of course we had no way of anticipating our men would shoot each other in the fog."

Operation *Cottage* inspired much sardonic commentary. Governor Gruening declared, "The battle for Alaska has ended ... and it may be reasonably contended the Japanese won it." Buckner observed, "To attract maximum attention, it's hard to find anything more effective than a great big, juicy, expensive mistake." *Time* magazine dubbed Kiska a JANFU – "Joint Army Navy (Foul)-Up." Across the Pacific, Japanese radio mocked the Americans for the embarrassing *Cottage* fiasco, apparently overlooking Churchill's ominous aphorism, "Wars are not won by evacuations."

August 1943 – Rockwell's Cottage invasion fleet masses at Adak, the finest anchorage in an Aleutian chain relatively poor in harbors. In 1911, Alfred Thayer Mahan had suggested coaling the US battle fleet at Kiska en route to Japan. The Aleutians always appealed to armchair strategists like Mahan who had never personally visited the region. (World War II Database)

US landing ships bring Allied troops ashore at Kiska during Operation *Cottage*, August 15–17, 1943. Colonel Eareckson orbited overhead in a B-24, sarcastically offering over the radio to donate a case of Scotch to whoever found the first Japanese. With the exception of Butler himself, the US Eleventh Air Force overwhelmingly believed Kiska had long been evacuated. (Time Life Pictures/ US Navy/The LIFE Picture Collection/Getty Images)

AFTERMATH

After *Cottage*, DeWitt, Buckner, and Kinkaid immediately pressed to invade the Kuriles, defended by an estimated 13,500 Japanese troops. Dewitt forwarded a plan to invade Paramushiro with 54,000 troops already in-theater; Buckner brazenly urged going "full blast" with 146,000 troops and three carrier task groups to force a "showdown action" against the Home Islands. However, MacArthur's and Spruance's simultaneous Southwest Pacific and Central Pacific offensives ultimately precluded a third North Pacific drive – there were limits even to American material power. Administratively, the Alaska Department was detached from Western Defense Command on November 1, 1943, but its strength fell from a post-*Cottage* peak of 152,000 personnel to 60,000 in 1945 and eventually 19,000 by 1946.

The USAAF's first post-*Cottage* Kuriles raid on September 11, 1943 was a disaster. Of seven B-24s and 12 B-25s, three were shot down and seven interned in the Soviet Union. USAAF raids were suspended until 1944. However, the Central Pacific's sunny Marianas, once captured, provided nearly the perfect B-29 base; ultimately, no B-29s ever staged from the Aleutians. Beginning in 1944, FAW-4 commenced the "Empire Express" bombing raids against the Kuriles that lasted through 1945. Vice Admiral Frank Jack Fletcher replaced the promoted Kinkaid as North Pacific Area commander on October 11, 1943. Now a backwater haven for obsolete Omaha-class cruisers, Fletcher's North Pacific Force first shelled the Kuriles in early 1944 and maintained North Pacific sweeps and bombardments through war's end.

The Aleutians campaign had inflicted comparatively little material damage on Japan: Between June 10, 1942 and August 15, 1943, Japan lost nine merchantmen, three destroyers, and five submarines in the Aleutians, with another four destroyers heavily damaged. Total Japanese naval and military personnel losses were 3,951. Including the merchant marine, some 5,100 Japanese had died in the Aleutians and in North Pacific waters. However, Operation *AL*'s original frittering away of strength in the North Pacific at the expense of the Midway *Schwerpunkt* was inexcusable, prompting US Secretary of the Navy Frank Knox's searing observation, "Japan was either unable to understand modern war or not qualified to take part in it." Every IJN warship, freighter, and gallon of fuel wasted in Alaskan waters between June 1942 and May 1943 would have been better employed at Midway or Guadalcanal, where American defeat was only narrowly staved off many times. More broadly, the IJN's consistently unsuccessful Aleutian relief attempts reveal the underlying fatal flaw in Japan's entire "Outer Defense

Sphere" Pacific grand strategy. Finally, after June 1942, IGHQ notably lacked the Americans' operational urgency, being consistently outworked, outmaneuvered, and outfought.

However, the US reconquest also proved a strategic dead end; the Aleutians remained "stepping stones to nowhere." Rockwell aide Robert Dennison explained irrational American motives best: "It was United States territory. That's something you don't do. You don't come over and grab some of our land. So we had to take it back regardless of strategy. We couldn't just let them sit there."

American pride demanded extravagantly disproportionate resources by the campaign's climax – 144,000 US personnel to 8,500 Japanese. Between June 1942 and August 1945, US aircraft in the North Pacific flew 8,108 combat sorties, dropped 4,630 tons of bombs, and destroyed 118 Japanese aircraft, while losing 480 US planes. Total Japanese aircraft losses to all causes were 269. However, by 1944, comparative theater strengths had reversed; relatively few American combat resources would tie up 80,000 Japanese troops and 500 Japanese aircraft defending the Kuriles against an invasion that never came.

Attu was Japan's first officially sanctioned Gyokusai, a surreal Japanese romanticism roughly translated "beautifully shattered jewel." Euphemistically, Gyokusai demanded the deliberate annihilation of an overwhelmed Japanese defense rather than its capitulation. Before Attu, there had been no firm policy of defeated Japanese garrisons being expected to self-immolate merely to save national face. For the first time, the United States had been required to virtually exterminate every Japanese on an island in order to secure it. As Japan's Pacific situation collapsed, it would unfortunately be Attu, not Kiska, IGHQ would be forced to emulate. From late 1943, almost every US-assaulted island would fight virtually to the last man.

Present-day historians' frequent claims the 1942–43 Aleutian campaign was somehow overlooked by wartime America are unfounded. Hollywood, *Time*, *Life*, *Newsweek*, *Reader's Digest*, and *The Saturday Evening Post* all devoted significant media coverage; John Huston, Robert Sherrod, Dashiell Hammett, Gore Vidal, and other luminaries reported on the theater. A wartime poll found only 21 percent of Americans could find Hawaii on a map, but 73 percent could peg the Aleutians. Indeed, the lurid vision of Japanese boots trampling on American soil naturally sold well with an anxious wartime public.

Yet the Aleutian campaign's many American embarrassments, miserable conditions, and – by August 1945 – clear strategic irrelevance to final American victory inspired its quick fade from public consciousness. US veterans returned less nostalgic and outspoken about their dreary Alaska service. American culture values clarity of purpose, decisive action, glamorous heroics, and easily romanticized imagery – ideals which ascribe easily to American campaigns across history-rich Western Europe and the Pacific's alluring, sun-drenched tropical isles. They do not greatly lend themselves to describing the remote and gloomy Aleutians.

THE BATTLEFIELDS TODAY

Alaska's wartime military boom proved permanent. The postwar specter of Soviet atomic bombs delivered over the North Pole made Alaska more strategically vital to American national security than ever before. World War II increased Alaska's national visibility and provided $1 billion of federally funded infrastructure, inspiring Alaskans to vote for statehood in 1946. Complex national politics concerning party, regional, and racial issues tied to potential civil rights legislation delayed Congressional approval for 12 years. Alaska finally became the 49th state on January 3, 1959. The 1968 discovery of the massive Prudhoe Bay Oil Field and subsequent 1977 completion of the Trans-Alaska Pipeline System would fundamentally transform Alaskan society.

With a population over 4,000, Unalaska (Dutch Harbor) hosts daily commercial flights and is easily the most accessible Aleutian battlefield. Unalaska museums include the Aleutian World War II Visitor Center and the Museum of the Aleutians. Farther west, US federal protection and the islands' own remoteness combine to make the Aleutians among the best protected, most undisturbed World War II battlefields anywhere to be found. Numerous sites from the campaign are listed on the National Register of Historic Places and some have been designated National Historic Landmarks. Kiska, Attu, and a B-24 crash site on Atka were included in the multistate World War II Valor in the Pacific National Monument established in 2008. While Adak and Atka host small populations, neither Kiska nor Attu have been inhabited since the closure of Attu's USCG station in August 2010; Kiska and Attu are now part of the Alaska Maritime National Wilderness and require prior authorization to visit.

A 1980s view of NAS Dutch Harbor/Fort Mears, taken by the Historic American Building Survey. The subject in this photo was the Quonset-style "Pacific Huts" in the foreground, erected during the 1942–43 Aleutian campaign and since torn down. Modern-day Dutch Harbor is now one of the top fishing ports in the world, with an annual harvest over $1 billion. (Library of Congress, HABS AK,1-UNAK,2-J-)

SELECT BIBLIOGRAPHY

Official/semi-official histories

Center of Military History, *CMH Pub 72-6 Aleutian Islands; the U.S. Army Campaigns of World War II*, Center of Military History, U.S. Army, Washington, DC, 1992

Conn, Stetson, Engelman, Rose C., and Fairchild, Byron, *Guarding the United States and its Outposts*. US Army Center for Military History, 1964

Craven, Wesley F., and Cate, James L. (eds.), *The Pacific: Guadalcanal to Saipan, August 1942 to July 1944*. Office of the US Air Force, 1950

——, *The Army Air Forces in World War II: Plans & Early Operations January 1939 to August 1942*, Office of Air Force History, United States, 1983

Dziuban, Stanley, *Military Relations Between the US and Canada 1939–1945*, US Department of the Army, Office of the Chief of Military History, 1959

Mitchell, Robert J., Tyng, Sewell T., and Drummond, Nelson L., *The Capture of Attu as Told by the Men Who Fought There*, Infantry Journal, Inc., 1944

Morison, Samuel Eliot, *Aleutians, Gilberts, and Marshalls, June 1942–April 1944*, Naval Institute Press, 2011

Office of Naval Intelligence, *Combat Narratives: The Aleutians Campaign June 1942–August 1943*, Washington, DC, 1945

Parker, Frederick D., *A Priceless Advantage: U.S. Navy Communications Intelligence and the Battles of the Coral Sea, Midway, and the Aleutians*, National Security Agency, Center for Cryptological History, 1993

Post Headquarters, Camp Earle, Alaska, *Short History of the Battle of Attu*, 1945

Orders/reports

Military History Section, Headquarters, Army Forces Far East, *Japanese Monograph No. 88: Aleutian Naval Operations March 1942–February 1943*, 1960

United States Strategic Bombing Survey, *The Campaigns of the Pacific War*, 1946

——, *USSBS No. 97: Interrogations of Japanese Officials – Carrier Aircraft Attack on Dutch Harbor*, 10 October 1945

——, *USSBS No. 98: Interrogations of Japanese Officials – Aleutian Campaign Seaplane Operations, the Naval Battle of the Komandorski Islands, and the Defense of the Kuriles*, 20–23 October 1945

——, *USSBS No. 99: Interrogations of Japanese Officials – Japanese Occupation of Kiska, the Kiska Garrison, and Operation in the Kuriles*, 22 October 1945

——, *USSBS No. 100: Interrogations of Japanese Officials – Aleutian Campaign – Japanese Flying Boat Operations in the Aleutians*, 9 October 1945

——, *USSBS No. 101: Interrogations of Japanese Officials – Aleutian Campaign – Planning and Operations through November 1942*, 11 October 1945

Updegraff, William, *Report on Bombing of Dutch Harbor, Commanding Officer*, 17 July 1942

Yamamoto, Isoroku, *Combined Fleet Operation Order No. 1*, 5 November 1941*Diaries/letters*

House, Charles, "Letter to Cdr. Neil F. O'Connor, USN, Naval War College."

Tatsuguchi, Paul Nobuo, Personal diary (trans. HQ Landing Force Office of ACX2 G-2 Massacre Valley, Attu Island), 1943

Articles/essays

Bishop, John, "My Speed Zero," *The Saturday Evening Post*, February 5, 1944

Hosaka, Mosakasu (trans. Szasz, Rodney J.) *Thoughts on the Sacrifice [Gyokusai] of the Attu Garrison*, 2007

Johnson, Robert L., Jr, *Aleutian Campaign, World War II: Historical Study and Current Perspective*, 1992

Books

Chandonnet, Fern, (ed.), *Alaska at War 1941–1945: The Forgotten War Remembered*, University of Alaska Press, Fairbanks, Alaska, 2008

Cloe, John Haile, *The Aleutian Warriors: A History of the 11th Air Force and Fleet Air Wing 4*, Pictorial Histories Publishing Co. and Anchorage Chapter – Air Force Association, Missoula, Montana, 1990

Coyle, Brandon, *War on our Doorstep: The Unknown Campaign on North America's West Coast*, Heritage House Publishing, 2010

Fuchida, Mitsuo, and Okumiya, Masatake, *Midway: The Battle that Doomed Japan*, Ballantine Books, 1982

Garfield, Brian, *The Thousand-Mile War: World War II in Alaska and the Aleutians*, Bantam Books, 1982

Goldstein, Donald M., and Dillon, Katherine V., *The Williwaw War: The Arkansas National Guard in the Aleutians in World War II*, The University of Arkansas Press, 1992

Lorelli, John A., *The Battle of the Komandorski Islands*, US Naval Institute Press, Annapolis, Maryland, 1984

Miller, Edward S., *War Plan Orange: The U.S. Strategy to Defeat Japan 1897–1945*, US Naval Institute Press, Annapolis, Maryland, 1991

Parshall, Jonathan, and Tully, Anthony, *Shattered Sword: The Untold Story of the Battle of Midway*, Potomac Books, Dulles, Virginia, 2005

Perras, Galen Roger, *Stepping Stones to Nowhere: The Aleutian Islands, Alaska, and American Military Strategy, 1867–1945*, University of British Columbia Press, Vancouver, British Columbia, 2003

Sato, Kazumasa (trans. Szasz, Rodney J.), *Gyokusai no Shima*, 2004

Willmott, H.P., *The Barrier and the Javelin: Japanese and Allied Pacific Strategies February to June 1942*, US Naval Institute Press, Annapolis, Maryland, 2008

Films

Huston, J. (Director), *Report from the Aleutians* [Motion picture], United States: US Army Signal Corps, 1943

Websites

http://www.ibiblio.org/hyperwar/
http://combinedfleet.com/
http://www.pwencycl.kgbudge.com/
http://aleutians.hlswilliwaw.com/
http://www.kadiak.org/
https://shatteredjewels.wordpress.com/
http://pacific.valka.cz/
http://www.navsource.org/
https://ww2db.com/
http://www.oocities.org/tempelhof.geo/
http://canadianheroes.org/
http://www.researcheratlarge.com/

INDEX

References to illustrations are in bold; captions are in brackets.